Zikrayat

Zikrayat

Eight Jewish Women Remember Egypt

NAYRA ATIYA

The American University in Cairo Press

Cairo New York

First published in 2020 by
The American University in Cairo Press
113 Sharia Kasr el Aini, Cairo, Egypt
One Rockefeller Plaza, New York, NY 10020
www.aucpress.com

Dar el Kutub No. 10592/19
ISBN 978 977 416 955 7

Dar el Kutub Cataloging-in-Publication Data

Atiya, Nayra
    Zikrayat: Eight Jewish Women Remember Egypt / Nayra Atiya.
    Cairo: The American University in Cairo Press, 2020.
    p.   cm.
    ISBN 978 977 416 955 7
    1.   Autobiography
    2.   Atiya, Nayra—Diaries
    920

1 2 3 4 5   24 23 22 21 20

Designed by Fatiha Bouzidi
Printed in the United Kingdom

For Melissa Solomon and for Eglal Errera,
friends over the years, women of courage, women
of the book. And to Asma, whose spirit lives on.

But think on me when it shall be well with thee, and shew kindness, I pray thee, unto me, and make mention of me unto Pharaoh, and bring me out of this house.

—Genesis 40:14

Contents

Foreword

by Andrea B. Rugh

Although the history of kings and rulers is unequivocally fascinating, I think we are also hungry for the narrative history of ordinary people . . . If history fails to represent all of us, it is not because historians are not interested, but because they lack the primary documents of so-called minor characters in history (Min Jin Lee, Pachinko 2017).[1]

History tends to be good at describing events of turbulent periods, even while missing the personal traumas of people living through them. This is due less to disinterest than it is to a lack of information to complete the picture.

So it is with the history of the Jews who were compelled to leave Egypt in the late 1940s, 1950s, and 1960s. Many people know parts of these events, but few know the actual conditions at different times that contributed to the exodus, or the effects on individuals and families. As time goes by and people die, or their memories fade, it becomes much harder to learn about their experiences.

Publishing the recollections of that period is especially urgent in this second decade of the twenty-first century, as mass migrations take place around the world. What do the experiences of Egyptian Jews tell us about people's feelings upon migration to a new land, or their feelings many years after the move? What reasons finally propelled Jews in Egypt to leave? How did they accomplish their departures once the decision was made? How similar or different were their experiences? What emotions did they feel looking back on their lives in Egypt or their lives in the diaspora? What was it like for those who visited Egypt years later? Did they feel a connection to the land of their birth?

Nayra Atiya's stories of Egyptian Jews take us a step further in filling the gap. The stories as told to Nayra fell on particularly sensitive ears, as she was herself a young girl growing up in the Egypt at the time, albeit in the Coptic community with its own set of minority experiences. She uses her knowledge of the time and place to fill out details when raconteurs abbreviated them, or took for granted her knowledge of what they were describing. She has taken other liberties to make the text more readable, such as ordering the sequence of events and strengthening the story line when her informants take extended detours. The result is a charming telling of stories that inevitably have their emotional highs and lows.

The stories suggest parallel themes in the lives of New York Jews who emigrated from Egypt and told Nayra their stories in the decade starting with 1987—roughly twenty to forty years after their departures—and yet each tells a distinctly different story, at least partly because tensions surrounding 'foreign' communities changed during different periods. A short history helps explain the circumstances that led to such different experiences for the Jews who left Egypt, and in particular the eight women Nayra met and interviewed in New York.

The short history

Most Westerners have a sketchy knowledge of the Jewish exodus from Arab lands in the twentieth century, but few know that the reasons for leaving differed over the decades. In addition, few understand what prompted 'indigenous' Egyptians to turn on groups that for so long had been an integral part of their community. They may not be aware, for example, that the growing hostility toward foreigners in the 1920s and 1930s that culminated in the expulsion of the British decimated not only the Jewish community but others, such as the Greeks. After independence in 1952, the pace of the expulsions accelerated during Nasser's presidency, with reforms meant to develop an Egyptian middle class and reduce economic inequalities through expanded employment opportunities, land redistribution, and sequestration of the assets of the wealthy. 'Foreign' assets were an easy target for Nasser in his efforts to level the playing field for the Egyptian masses.

Although small communities of Jews, numbering around two thousand, existed in Egypt well before the nineteenth century, it was not until Muhammad Ali's tenure (1805–48) that economic opportunities, especially in trade, attracted large numbers of Jews and other migrants from around the eastern shores of the Mediterranean. A second wave of migrants appeared in the early twentieth century, again attracted by economic opportunities and a desire to escape persecution in the countries of their origins. In one memoir, the author's father, born in Aleppo, Syria, was brought as an infant to Egypt. His father died shortly after their arrival but his mother kept "her Halab culture" in Egypt, giving the family a sense of superiority over local culture.

The years 1900 to 1937 under British occupation were a 'golden age' for the migrants. Many maintained their foreign passports, either because they and other non-Muslim foreigners found it difficult to become naturalized citizens, or because these documents gave them protected status. By the late 1930s and 1940s, the tolerance extended to them as foreigners began to fade, and by the late 1940s, attacks on Egyptian Jews intensified because of their presumed links to Zionism. The capitulations system that had previously given foreigners legal protection under their own consular jurisdictions was abolished in 1949, putting them under the jurisdiction of the Egyptian court system.[2]

In the early part of the twentieth century, some Jews motivated by a desire for social justice and cooperation between Egyptians of differing faiths became active in leftist causes. One prominent example was Henri Curiel (1914–78), an Egyptian-born Jew who led the communist Democratic Movement for National Liberation until he was expelled from Egypt in 1950 on trumped-up charges of Zionism. He was in fact a vocal anti-Zionist.

Tensions further intensified with growing Egyptian hostility toward British occupation, and by extension toward all non-Muslim 'foreigners' who had privileges under the British occupation. The Jews, as well as other non-Muslim groups throughout this period, were seen primarily as 'foreigners,' even though many were born and had lived in the country all their lives. Even Coptic Christians, who claimed Egyptian origins back as far as pharaonic times, were linked to outsiders as a result of British and American missionary activity, and through considerable Western funding.

Historians credit a series of wars and political events from the late 1940s until the late 1960s with forcing the departures of Jews and other 'foreigners' from Egypt. For Jews, the first was the Arab–Israeli War of 1948 that culminated in the creation of the state of Israel. Of the roughly seventy-five thousand Jews who lived in Egypt at the time, about twenty thousand left after 1948–49. In this first major exodus from Egypt and other Muslim countries, many of the educated left because they were inspired by the idea of a Jewish homeland, while the rest were mainly poorer Jews seeking economic opportunities in Israel. Those with major assets mostly stayed in Egypt, hoping the situation would improve.

About five thousand more Jews left Egypt between 1952 and 1956 for various reasons. One was the loss of public-sector jobs after independence, as Nasser sought to compensate for the overrepresentation of non-Muslims in these positions under the British. Nasser's nationalization of properties, industries, and services also hit Jewish populations hard economically when their assets were seized.

The failed Lavon Affair in 1954 increased internal resentment against Jews. In this plot, an Israeli team placed bombs in public places to make it appear like a Muslim plot, the intent being to encourage Britain to keep troops in Egypt for security purposes. The plot was revealed and suspicions deepened around the possibility of local Jews becoming further involved in subversive acts.

Jewish migration from Egypt peaked again after the Suez crisis in 1956 when, in response to Nasser nationalizing the Suez Canal, British, French, and Israeli forces attacked Egypt. The United States quickly intervened at the United Nations on Egypt's behalf and the foreign forces withdrew. But the event aggravated tensions between the government and local residents from the countries involved. Between November 1956 and March 1957, fourteen thousand Jews emigrated, and over the next ten years nineteen thousand more left Egypt. During the crisis, over one thousand Jews were arrested and five hundred of their businesses were confiscated. At the same time a statement was read in mosques saying Jews were Zionists and therefore enemies of the state. The bank accounts of many Jews were seized and thousands were told to leave. French and British residents also had their assets seized, along with members of the Greek and Italian communities who were labeled 'foreign,' even though they had lived for generations in Egypt. The Jews, however, bore the brunt of the hostility because of their assumed links to Israel, even though many of them had opposed the formation of the Zionist state.

By 1957, only fifteen thousand Jews remained in Egypt. And by 1960, the American Embassy reported that the remainder also had a strong desire to leave, but that for them it was more a question of restricted economic opportunities than mistreatment at the hands of the government. Of those leaving Egypt at the time, half went to Israel and the other half to France and North and South America, while smaller numbers went elsewhere. In the end, of the nine-hundred thousand Jews who left Arab and Muslim countries, six-hundred thousand settled in Israel and three-hundred thousand went to France and the US. The push factors in Egypt were persecution, political instability, poverty, and finally, after 1956, overt expulsion. The pull factors were Zionist sympathies and, for those with appropriate documents, better economic opportunities and stability in Europe and America.

The final blow to the dwindling Jewish populations came after the 1967 Arab–Israeli War, when Jews were again viewed as a fifth column by Egyptian authorities. They were detained and tortured, and their homes were confiscated. By this time only a few Jews were left, mostly the elderly or those married to local Egyptians. In the latest count (2017), the community only consisted of eighteen members (twelve in Alexandria and six in Cairo). Nineteen synagogues remain, with several of those slated for historic preservation in 2019, according to local authorities.

Needless to say, and regardless of conditions, migration was painful for those who left, especially those who felt they had contributed significantly to the multicultural community that characterized Egypt in the early twentieth century.

Nayra's histories

Where do Nayra's raconteurs fit into this picture? Do their stories reveal the details of the lives of 'minor characters' that history so often fails to provide? Her sample of eight Jewish women constitutes only a tiny percentage of those who left Egypt, albeit an important one. It does not, for example, tell us about poorer Jews, such as those living in Harat al-Yahud (the Jewish Quarter) in Cairo, many of whom emigrated to Israel. The stories do, however, tell us a great deal about the middle- and upper-class Jews who migrated to the Americas and Europe, where appropriate documents and connections were crucial. Their stories give us important insights into a group that took this particular route out of Egypt, giving us a sense of their lives in Egypt before their departure and their important contributions to the multicultural societies of Cairo and Alexandria.

Alexandria was the setting for many of their lives. All who lived there describe the wonderful multicultural polyglot atmosphere of the time—the foods, smells, and sophistication of the society—before the troubles started. It's hard to overstate the magical quality of 'Alex' during its heyday in the 1920s, 1930s, and early 1940s. Lawrence Durrell's *Alexandria Quartet* describes it best: as a city large enough to accommodate different lifestyles and 'foreign' communities—Greek, Italian, French, and Jewish—yet with each retaining its distinct identity. Even while enjoying this separateness of family and religious life, affluent members of the different communities shed their identities in clubs, restaurants, and hotels like the Cecil, where, over drinks and good food, and speaking a mix of languages, they mingled with little regard for ethnic or religious background. In the early twentieth century these communities looked to Paris, London, and Rome for their models, rather than Cairo or destinations farther south.

The downside of keeping separate identities was the ease with which they were targeted when Egyptian attitudes changed. Their 'foreignness' was accentuated by relative affluence, protected status under the British, and general disdain for local society that stirred resentment in local populations. They were also identifiable through their residential addresses, names, religious practices, and places of worship. What had been interesting but unimportant differences took on significance with Egypt's growing nationalism and involvement in international events. In the end, the private boundaries that set them apart—Jewish, French, Greek, or Italian—made it easier to oppress and ultimately expel them.

In numerous ways, Nayra's eight narrators embody the personal details only abstractly described in the history books. They were children or grandchildren of generations who migrated to Egypt from around or near the Mediterranean—Austria, Romania, France, Iraq, Italy, Russia, Spain, and Syria—to escape economic privations and persecution or, in one case, a family conflict. Most kept foreign passports for reasons already noted—French, Austrian, Italian, and earlier the Ottoman laissez-passer documents issued by the Egyptian government. Some bought Italian or Portuguese passports when the need arose. Family income earners found work in banking, cotton brokering, textile manufacturing and sales, jewelry or clock making, and furniture or toy importing. One was a button maker, another a construction contractor, and several engaged in real estate businesses.

With the exception of Ester, who lived in the modest Daher neighborhood, these middle- and upper-class Jews resided in relatively upscale communities near other Jewish families. They lived in elegant apartments furnished in European styles, with servants, fine foods, memberships in elite clubs, and summers spent on the beach near Alexandria or on visits to Europe. Their children attended private Jewish schools or ones founded by Europeans, while the richer ones employed European nannies to supervise the children's after-school hours. During the week the parents mixed freely with Egyptians and foreigners who were their customers, suppliers, contractors, and social acquaintances.

At their tony private schools, the Jewish children's friends included children of affluent families from Egyptian, Greek, French, and Italian communities who were practicing Muslims, Copts, Protestants, and Catholics. Their classes were held in foreign languages—mainly French and English, which were the lingua franca of the upper classes, but with some specializing in Italian and German. At home they mixed these languages and added languages of their own communities.[3] Few learned Arabic other than what was necessary to communicate with servants—but rarely the skill of reading and writing Arabic fluently. For these 'foreigners,' European languages were key to the sophisticated lifestyle they aspired to. Only Mimi and Chaviva claimed to know Arabic well, the first because her father felt it helped his career and so brought a sheikh to teach his children, and Chaviva because her parents lived in the countryside among Egyptians.

Religion and ethnic origin were personal matters that didn't interfere with day-to-day social relationships or their private lives. For Jews, family obligations meant dinners together, observing the Jewish sabbath and other traditions, and ensuring their children married within the Jewish community. Many generously funded schools and hospitals and contributed to charitable organizations, such as the orphanage La Goutte de Lait. In all this, they were not unlike Christian and Muslim communities.

Even though some of the narrators reported tensions growing during the early 1940s, it was not until the late 1950s and early 1960s that most of these families left Egypt. With the exception of Maaya, who left in 1949, inspired by her interest in a Jewish homeland, others left fairly late—1961 for Ester and 1960 for Adina. The latter confirmed that by the time her family left, most Jews were gone. By 1962, Nasser made it clear that all Jews and other non-Muslim foreigners should go, and was harassing them. In the late 1950s, Chaviva's family's land was sequestered during Nasser's land reforms (which also affected Coptic and Muslim landowners). Nevertheless, they remained in Egypt until 1964, when they went first to

Israel and then, two years later, to New York when they found Israel too "rugged" for their liking.

Those who married outside the faith to local Egyptians could stay, such as Vida's brother, who married into the royal family and became a Muslim. Other prominent men, such as Boutros Boutros-Ghali, Egypt's foreign minister and later United Nations Secretary-General, married Jewish women, suggesting that Jewishness as a religion or social category was not the problem. In one case mentioned by a narrator, a Jewish girl was sent abroad by her parents when King Faruq, the famous womanizer, paid too much attention to her.

Most of the narrators confirm that their families left for economic reasons, often after their assets were seized. But in one case, when a child was imprisoned because she was a member of a Jewish organization plotting acts of subversion, the family agreed to leave as a condition of her release. Some families delayed leaving because of sick or elderly family members who couldn't travel. Those who left during later periods had harsh restrictions placed on their departure: they were forced to give up their assets, and allowed to take only a small amount of cash and a few possessions. They also had to agree never to return.

One senses a complex relationship between Jews and local Egyptian residents. While Jews mixed easily with affluent Egyptians who shared their love of European lifestyles, the relationships with those who served them as house servants and workers were more complicated. In some cases, strong emotional attachments characterized their relationships, but in others class tensions appear to have existed. Mimi noted that their servants, who had seemed so devoted before the revolution, began taking liberties after 1952, with one telling her the way their family lived was wrong. Only Chaviva's cotton-growing rural family mixed with Egyptians on their own terms and spoke their own language. The resentments of working-class Egyptians finally spilled over, and ultimately led to events culminating in Egyptian independence. The disdain of foreign communities for Egyptian culture had a bearing on these developments. Even though this did not excuse the government's heavy-handed treatment of Jews after 1956, it surely fueled local resentments and ultimately contributed to their expulsion.

As Mimi says, Egypt was like heaven on earth until the 1940s, welcoming warmly as it did survivors of the Holocaust. She eventually left to France, but Egypt never left her heart, and she would have stayed if the Jews had been wanted. She became a Zionist but not because she was against Egypt.

In *Zikrayat*, as in her first two books, *Khul-Khaal: Five Egyptian Women Tell their Stories* and *Shahaama: Five Egyptian Men Tell Their Stories*, Nayra writes with a fluidity and grace that captures the essence of the women's stories, their personalities, and the complex atmospherics of the times in Egypt. The book provides insights into a time and place—a glimpse into a long-lost world—and the painful necessity of leaving it. The stories contribute to a growing corpus of documents and memoirs about this turbulent period. But in the end, they are not just Jewish stories, they are stories about all migrants who feel compelled to leave the land of their birth and make a new life in another country. In this case it is noteworthy that the women do not dwell as much on their Jewishness as they do on their lives in Egypt. The reader is left with the feeling that Egypt had the most to lose when these communities departed.

The stories begin to fill the gap in history by giving us the personal details we long to hear. They are about a time and experience we need to know more about.

Andrea B. Rugh *is an author and anthropologist who has lived and worked in the Middle East for several decades. She has shared many adventures with Nayra Atiya over forty years of friendship, some of which are recounted in her book,* Simple Gestures, A Cultural Journey into the Middle East *(Nebraska: Potomac Books, University of Nebraska Press, 2009).*

Preface

It was a joy and a privilege to meet the eight women whose stories you are about to read. We became friends and were enthusiastic about sharing what we remembered of our lives in Egypt, a land we had all loved and left, some by choice, others under duress. The fact that they were Jewish and I was born and raised in the Coptic Church, the ancient Christian church of Egypt, made no difference to the warmth with which we related and the pleasure we took in each other's company as we traded stories. We found commonalities and differences in our experiences as minorities in Egypt and noted them with curiosity and tolerance. We had fun.

I left Egypt as a child of ten in the 1950s. My friends migrated as adults during the 1940s, 1950s, and 1960s. When we met in New York City, they were well established and at home in the United States. I was too. We intuited each other's backgrounds and points of reference, and quickly recognized one another's manner of speaking and gestures, sharing food and experiences. We shared outings, meals, friends, and family, celebrating and grieving with one another. It felt natural, as if we had known each other all our lives. Perhaps this is due to having literally and symbolically walked on common ground. Egypt seemed always at the heart of our conversations. In sharing memories, we brought the land of our childhoods to life. Memories nurtured our friendships and fed our stories.

Maaya, Mimi, Ester, Chaviva, Pilar, Vida, Ariadne, and Adina came from middle- and upper-middle-class Jewish families living in Cairo and Alexandria. One grew up in the region of the Nile Delta, on a farm. These stories unfold in mid-twentieth-century Egypt, ending when the women and their families emigrate or are expelled in the time of the exodus.

One mentions a brother who stayed behind, having converted to Islam to marry a Muslim woman. Like him, the few who stayed after 1967 did so because of marriages or intimate associations with members of other Egyptian communities.

Having recorded and transcribed these stories over a period of a few years, I gave the taped recordings to a Jewish friend to archive, and laid the transcripts aside when I left New York for Salt Lake City, Utah, to care for my aging and ailing mother. The box of transcripts followed me, was lost, then found and opened as one would a forgotten box of treasure. I reread them and was moved to revive the stories by way of remembering and honoring my friends, most of whom have now died. Hopefully their voices, entwined with mine, will add to a growing body of memoirs of Egypt's children.

Rereading the raw transcripts, I soon realized that they needed tweaking. I set to work organizing and building them into narratives, supplementing them with details broadly hinted at but not replicated word for word by the storytellers. I fleshed out certain parts with details and general historical information. Vida, for example, had once mentioned in conversation the names of prominent and not-so-prominent Jews she knew or had read about who made their mark on the "tapestry that is Egypt," as she put it. I included some of those names, adding detail.

I have adjusted storylines, adding context and clarifying ambiguities as needed to enhance the flow of the narratives. In one instance, I wrote a dialogue based on the transcripts at hand as well as notes jotted down over years of friendship with Maaya, reconstructing a conversation she had as a very young girl with her father, a teacher.

I suppose you might call this method of rendering another's story impressionistic, and you would be right. These eight stories are true stories, however, even if reconstructed to give them the fluidity the transcripts lacked, and even if I have tossed in snippets from my own hamper of memories to round them out. I made every effort, however, to keep from talking above or over the voices of the storytellers, though I am surely present between the lines. As with painting a portrait, something of the artist is revealed. When one of the storytellers mentioned going to see black-and-white movies starring the Italian comic Toto but could not remember where in Alexandria, I added that it was at the Cinéma Gaité in Ibrahimiya where, as a child, I had seen Toto, as well as my first Tarzan movie with Johnny Weissmuller. She might have, too.

It is the essence of these eight women's personalities and lives that I have endeavored to express through the filter of their memories and mine, weaving scattered reminiscences into narrative. As I put the clasp on this necklaces of stories, I am thinking about how Jewish tradition is built on a foundation of memory, *Zakar* or *Zakhor*.

In Deuteronomy 4:94 KJV (Sefer Devarim, the fifth book of the Torah) we read: "Only take heed to thyself, and keep thy soul diligently, lest thou forget the things which thine eyes have seen, and lest they depart from thy heart all the days of thy life."

Judaism, I have learned, invokes the faithful to carry in their hearts the commandment to remember, thus ensuring solidarity and continuity. In my *Shahaama: Five Egyptian Men Tell Their Stories*, Youssef Salman, the only Jewish storyteller of the five, explained this concept by posing a question: "Nayra, did not the Baal Shem Tov (founder of Hasidism) teach that forgetfulness leads to exile while remembrance is the secret of redemption?" His words have stayed with me through the years.

Remembering through word, deed, and ritual, while recounting their own stories, these women allude to their history as a people, especially to the exodus from Egypt celebrated in the course of the seder, the ritual service and ceremonial Passover dinner. One year, when invited to share, it fell upon me to read the following passage from the Haggadah, the text recited at the dinner table: "There arose in Egypt a Pharaoh who knew not of the good deeds that Joseph had done for that country. Thus he enslaved the Jews and made their lives harsh through servitude and humiliation. This is the basis for the Passover holiday which we commemorate with these different rituals tonight."

In remembering and recounting the exodus, Jews satisfy the double command to show and to see themselves and their people as having come forth from Egypt, out of Egypt, to freedom.

I hope that these mini memoirs will afford you a glimpse of a few Egyptian lives interlaced with snippets of the history and spirit of a people who once upon a time (and not just once) were an integral part of Egypt's story.

The great American poet and author Maya Angelou said, "There is no greater agony than bearing an untold story inside you." These eight women were eager to share their stories and were, I think, transformed as they remembered and spoke. In recounting their stories, they unburdened themselves, each leaving a small legacy for coming generations. In listening, I was transported to the source of my own memories. To tell and write these stories was satisfying and healing for us as women who had experienced being 'the other,' severed from the mother tree, planted in unfamiliar soil where we labored to take root and blend in. Telling our stories smoothed the way.

Nobel Laureate and Holocaust survivor Elie Wiesel (1928–2016) wrote: "I marvel at the resilience of the Jewish people. Their best characteristic is their desire to remember. No other people has such an obsession with memory."

In the spirit of remembering and recounting their stories, these women and I have shared details of our lives in Egypt and after Egypt, told one voice at a time, memory by memory. Our hope is to add a few nuggets to the ever-expanding body of memoirs of and by Egyptian Jews.

Acknowledgments

Thanks to so many Egyptian Jewish acquaintances, oral historians, memoirists, and friends, whose conversation and enthusiasm inspired the process of pulling these stories into a collection. And thank you most recently to Nadia Naqib from AUC Press for suggesting *zikrayat* (reminiscences) as a title.

Very special thanks to Andrea Rugh for years of walks, talks, inspiration, and shared adventures, and for tirelessly reviewing the manuscript and writing the introduction. Thanks to Mary Megalli for her friendship, her willingness to read and edit, for loudly grousing about too many commas and the proper use of *it's* and *its*. Her discreet support over the years is a gift. Shukran to Amina Megalli and Katrina Malkin for their affectionate, sparkling spirit and timely words of encouragement. Merci to Hannah Lola and Amina Love for their whimsical input, which kept me "light as a feather" while writing, and to the Wonder Buzz, my champion and teacher, who cleared the path of stones, reminding me to "keep a smile in it." Much appreciation to Michelle Slater for her strength of spirit along paths and years of 'goose migrations.' Gratitude to Michael Myjak for hands-on help at the computer, for the fun we have along the way, and for lovingly cheering me on. Last but not least, I wish to offer heartfelt thanks to my beloved family for growing up together, for all of the shared "expotitions," fun, sparks, creative and nurturing meals, and for always keeping lights on at a window, under a tent flap, at a porthole, or on a deck.

Shukran to all.

1

Vida

Meeting Vida

Vida and I met serendipitously in 1987. I had returned to the United States after an extended stay in Egypt, the land of my birth, and was looking to make a home in New York City. Friends suggested I would enjoy an exhibit at the Brooklyn Museum. It was there I saw Vida for the first time.

At the museum, I wandered around looking at sketches and paintings, and then stood before Mary Frank's sculpture of Persephone, her body composed of fragments of clay on a dais. It brought to mind the Egyptian goddess Isis, who found her slain husband in fragments, restored his broken body, and brought him back to life. As I was admiring this sculpture, Vida came up and stood gazing intently at it as well. I glanced at her and smiled.

Something about Vida seemed familiar, yet I could not define what it was exactly. She could have been one of my aunts. She carried herself with dignity and had a friendly, open countenance. Her big blue eyes sparkled with interest and energy. She wore a smart navy-blue pant suit and a cream silk blouse with a high neck to which she had pinned a brown scarab brooch set in gold. Vida's white hair shone under the lights. She was perfectly coiffed in a bouffant hairstyle that added an inch or two to her five feet. She walked gingerly in patent-leather orthopedic shoes, a large matching handbag hung over her arm. To me, this bag was distinctly in the style of bags I had seen my mother and aunts carrying, some of them created by 'Miss Egypt,' a family-owned business with an elegant shop at the Hilton Hotel in Cairo.

Why did Vida seem so familiar? Was it her body language, her ready smile, the scarab brooch, the bag, her countenance?

Have I seen this woman before? I wondered. Have we met? Maybe in Egypt?

My eyes must have been full of question marks because she caught my look and initiated a conversation as we moved around the sculpture. It is easy to speak to someone when they stir in us a sense of recognition, I thought.

Vida turned to me and with an accent similar to my mother's, who also rolled her r's, she asked, "Are you familiar with the work of Mary Frank? What an amazing Persephone!"

"Yes. Powerful," I responded, adding: "I was just thinking how this interpretation of Persephone reminds me of the Egyptian goddess Isis gathering fragments of her husband Osiris's broken body, making him whole again and returning him to life. Do you know this myth?"

Vida exclaimed, "Isis, of course! I grew up hearing it. May I ask where you are from?"

When I said I was Egyptian, she began to speak to me in a familiar mix of English, French, and Arabic, a hodgepodge some Egyptians are known to use simultaneously. And so began the friendship between Vida and I, which led to meeting members of her family, and to introductions to other Egyptian Jews, who befriended me and were happy to share their memories of Egypt and their stories.

Vida tells her story

The Jews of Egypt have always had a knack for taking the best of everything around them and enjoying it. Egypt was welcoming back then, and we enjoyed whatever the country had to offer. The Jews prospered in Egypt and we made good lives for ourselves: dressed well, traveled well, led the high life, worked hard, nurtured solid communities, built synagogues and schools, founded organizations, institutions, commercial establishments, and always remembered the less fortunate among us. The rich built and supported homes to benefit and aid the orphaned and the aging; generations of children grew up and succeeded after being raised in Jewish orphanages. Not only did the Jews make an impact in business, we did so in literary fields as well. Look at Ya'kub Sanu, a nineteenth-century satirist and playwright who was involved in the political and cultural life of Egypt and got away with criticizing Muslim customs and rulers. He was better known by his nickname Abu Naddara (he who wears glasses).

Among the Jewish families who distinguished themselves in Egypt, I am remembering the Suares, Menasce, Mosseri, Rolo, Cattaoui, Aghion, and Ada families, to name but a few. They made their mark on the Egypt I grew up in. They had an impact in many spheres, including agriculture, industry, commerce, finance, the political arena, and in their respective professions. Jacob Cattaoui, for example, was in charge of the financial affairs of the state under Khedive Abbas I, viceroy of Egypt in the 1840s and 1950s; Cattaoui's son was president of the Jewish community for forty years and funded the education and training of gifted youths; the Menasces were associated with many successful trading establishments and were prominent philanthropists as well, funding the Menasce Free Schools in Alexandria; the Mosseris were in banking since the 1800s. Nessim Mosseri was elected president of the Mixed Tribunal of Commerce and his son, Youssef, followed in his footsteps. Other members of the family were known for contributions to the development of cotton cultivation, its use and export. The Ada family was instrumental in the commercialization of cotton, and were key players in Egypt's railway administration. In the philanthropic tradition exhibited by Jews, they established a hospital and a home for the elderly in Alexandria. There were so many who gave so much to a country that ended up turning its back on all of us. It breaks my heart when I think of it. But enough of this.

Do you remember the neighborhood of Smouha? This upscale suburb was the brainchild of Joseph Smouha, a British Jew living in Egypt. It had its own tennis courts and golf courses, schools, hospitals, synagogues, mosques, and churches. There are many lesser-known figures, many probably forgotten today. I have sought them out. As I study Jewish history I discover names. For example, have you heard of Isaac Vaena, who exported onions, Egypt's third-largest crop? Or those Jews in the Delta region who established cotton gins and contributed to the booming Egyptian textile industry? Habib Aripol comes to mind. He set up a factory in Mansura and his heirs ran it until the 1960s when it was nationalized. Many prominent and not-so-prominent Jews were vital in weaving the tapestry that is Egypt and contributing richly to its development.

The Jews sank roots into Egypt. You can still see where we lived and flourished, where we made our mark, even if our communities are now decimated. Really, you need only look at synagogues and cemeteries to see proof of Jewish presence. Look at department stores still in business today that bear the names of their original owners—Cicurel, Oreco, Hannaux,

Ades, all Jews. We have contributed a lot to Egypt and yes, we also benefited greatly until we were thrown out. What a pity. It is Egypt's loss and ours. From time to time, I ask myself what Egypt would be like today had the Jews remained and continued to flourish. I wonder.

In the 1930s, Alexandria's Jewish community—the community I grew up in—numbered about twenty-five thousand. In Cairo, the numbers were greater and the community more diverse, both ethnically and socially. Some lived near the poverty line in the neighborhood of Harat al-Yahud (Alley of the Jews). This was not a world I knew.

I grew up in Alexandria in an atmosphere of luxury and leisure, among Jews who knew nothing of struggle until we left Egypt. Families of means such as ours had governesses, cooks, maids and chambermaids. These chambermaids, called camareras, were generally Italians from Gorizia. Once they established themselves in a family and their employment appeared to be secure, they brought other members of their families into service. It was thus that many Gorizian families were reconstituted in Egypt. In the early 1900s there was even a Rabbi Raphael Della Pergola, who was from Gorizia.

Wealthy Egyptian Jews were up to date on everything and they were very, very snobbish. They really knew how to live, how to make the most of life. I was once part of that group. You can ask now, "How did you ever come down to earth, Vida?" And I will tell you that I not only came down to earth, but I came down with a resounding thud when we were expelled from Egypt. We were uprooted, forced to leave with nothing but the clothes on our backs and a small suitcase of personal belongings. Everything we owned was confiscated.

We began to feel turbulence in our Jewish communities a decade before we were forced to leave Egypt, to abandon our homes, our synagogues and schools, our wealth, our way of life, our memories, the sacred ground where our dead are buried. Everything that was meaningful to us, everything that defined us was whisked away in the blink of an eye.

As I experienced rejection and heartbreak, I thought of my parents. Time and time again I invoked them, reciting a litany of regrets to them out loud, and thinking how lucky they were not to have witnessed such times. "My father and mother, you have been spared the pain of being cast out of your home and forced to abandon everything familiar and pleasant." I drew some comfort from unburdening my heart in this way.

My husband and I and our children were turned out of Egypt in the blink of an eye. We were given no choice, no time to prepare, no chance to come to terms with our plight. "Out, you! Go!" was the message clearly writ. And out we went. What to do when the full force of circumstance brings you to your knees? "Get up, dust off, and keep going," Mother used to say. And that is what we did.

We connected with family in New Jersey. They gave us a safe place to land and start over, but Monmouth County where they lived was too rich for us, as we'd been allowed to take nothing with us but a few dollars and a suitcase of clothes. We explored New York, and chose Brooklyn, where we found an apartment and began our American journey. We struggled the first few years but slowly made progress and built meaningful, satisfying lives. We had to forget the rich and easy way we lived in Egypt, but we found safety and satisfaction in New York and eventually did well and felt at home.

When we decided to quit New Jersey, my husband searched for and found an apartment in Brooklyn. Without hesitation, our families pitched in with the necessities to help us start housekeeping anew. They gave us furniture and assisted us in our move; they encouraged us and wished us well, letting us know all the while that they would support us in any way they could. "It takes efforts to start over, to adjust, to build again," a cousin said, "but you are strong and you will succeed, of this I am certain." She was right.

My husband soon started a business that eventually made us a comfortable living. We raised our children into successful, responsible adults and professionals, and when they married and moved to Long Island, they kept after us to move with them. We felt at home in Brooklyn and told them we were close enough to visit and spend the holidays together, but would remain where we were. Even after my husband died, I stayed. "Be active, be independent" is my motto and it has served me well. Of course, after my husband's death, I suffered the loneliness of the widow but refused to give in to my grief. "It's a life of purpose you must lead, Vida," I said to myself. And so I did, finding companionship among family and friends, always staying active. No dwelling on sadness for me, I thought as I woke every morning. I adopted my Catholic friend Catherine's Latin saying, "*vietato lamentarsi*" (complaining is forbidden), and I stayed busy.

When the apartment where the children grew up felt too big and I found it too hard to maintain, my children bought me a one-bedroom apartment and helped me to move. It took a while to get accustomed to a small space, but I have now. Actually, I felt liberated. I refer to my new digs as "cozy" and feel free to pursue interests outside the home. I am free as a bird. Less space, fewer possessions, and a simpler life have given me the gift of time—time to spend with friends, to learn, to teach, to volunteer, and to celebrate life. I am blessed with a family who visits me often and invites me to visit them, coming to pick me up in Brooklyn and driving me home. I do not drive, but I go out to Long Island with them for holidays, staying with each of my children a few days at a time. I make sure not to stay too long.

I have many interests. Chief among them is art. I use my gifts as an artist to enrich my life and the lives of others through teaching and creating handmade gifts. I offer painting and calligraphy classes at my local senior center, and raise money for them by making greeting cards and posters, and I always enjoy Torah and tea with my friends. No complaints!

In Egypt, my family lived in a twenty-two-room villa with a huge garden surrounding it, served by a generous staff, each with their well-defined duties in the household. Even now, more than half a century later, I remember their names and the Arabic word describing their jobs. How strange it is to consider that details from so long ago stay with you!

Our *ganayni* (gardener) was Mahmud, his assistant was Zaki. The *dada* (nanny) was Karima, and she had two aides, Aziza and Azza. The cook was Usta Fathi. *Usta* meant chef but also could mean chauffeur. Our driver was therefore Usta Kamel. We even had a gofer, a teenager I nicknamed Simsim, sesame seed, alluding to the tale of "Ali Baba and the Forty Thieves," which Mother read to us in French from a beautiful volume of 'One Thousand and One Nights.' He ran errands and did any little job he was told to do by the staff, including unlocking the garden gate in the morning. The gardener would call out to him, "*Iftah ya Simsim*" (Open sesame), the magic phrase by which the thieves opened a cave full of treasures.

Of our Egyptian servants, the one that stands out in my memory is our *sufragi*, a tall Nubian whose job was to serve at the table. He had the unusual name of Kerman. Was it his real name? I was never able to find out. My father trusted him, and when Kerman was not busy with home duties, he was charged with sensitive errands, such as taking sums of money to the bank. Kerman was tall, strikingly handsome, and always impeccably dressed in a gallabiya so bright that he seemed a streak of white light as he walked by. When serving at the table, his uniform was a striped kaftan tailored for him out of *shahi* (polished cotton) and a *tarboosh*.

Often servants were passed around the family. When my children were born, Dada Karima was sent to help me. She had come into my mother's service as a little girl and grew up in the family. When my children grew up, Dada took care of my younger brother's children. Mother sent Usta Fathi to me when I first got married. He had been in service with us for years and Mother trusted him to be steady and helpful to a new bride. That's how it was done.

Like so many Jews in Egypt, my father was in banking, and was also a cotton broker. We had an easy life and my mother raised us with little effort. Help was so available and affordable that it made it easy to have large families. Men followed religious teachings to the letter and did not use contraception. Were we not taught to be fruitful and multiply? In Judaism it is considered a *mitzvah*, a commandment or religious duty. This is why faithful Jewish families had so many children—as many as seventeen among our family and the members of our community. My father was one of fourteen children, my mother one of ten, and they had nine children themselves. Having so many children sometimes caused quite a mishmash, by which I mean that children were so widely spaced that the youngest barely knew the eldest. In some families, the eldest siblings might have died, left home, or emigrated before setting eyes on their youngest brothers or sisters. Sometimes nephews and nieces were older than their uncles and aunts. Adults calling children Auntie or Uncle caused a good deal of mirth. That's just the way it was and no one questioned the order of things.

In some Jewish families there were cousin marriages. This was practiced in order to keep wealth and property in the family. It is not a good thing. I grew up with two cousins born of such marriages. One had twisted limbs and another was simpleminded. The latter was close to my age and quite attached to me. He was sweet, smiled a lot, and remained a child until he died at the age of thirty.

I was born in Alexandria in 1915, the third daughter of Abraham Bekhor, who was the eldest son in his family, and Ariella Aharon, the eldest daughter in hers. It was customary in Jewish families to name the eldest boy after his paternal grandfather. Thus all male members of my father's family were named Abraham Bekhor or Bekhor Abraham, reversing the name of the grandfather and the great-grandfather with each generation.

My father's father was Bekhor Abraham. He was a whiz at finance and accumulated his wealth by serving as a financial advisor to Ismail Pasha, khedive of Egypt. His ancestors were originally from Spain. The family fled to France to escape persecution but my grandfather had his eye on Egypt. People were shivering in Europe, while Egypt was warm and welcoming, and this was where he wanted to live and die. He fell in love with Egypt and it was in Egypt that Bekhor Abraham met and married my great-grandmother. Unfortunately, there is little record of his life and even less of hers. One thing I am assuming is that he spoke Arabic as he was employed and trusted by Ismail Pasha, the ruler of Egypt. The story told is that the khedive assigned Abraham Bekhor the task of collecting Khorda (copper currency) and arranging for carts to transport it to the treasury, which is how it was apparently done in those days. In time, my ancestor earned a place in the khedive's inner circle and Bekhor Abraham altered his name to Bekhor Ibrahim in an effort to assimilate. He also adopted the Egyptian style of dress, donning the baggy pants, the *sirwal*, topped with a cummerbund. We had a photo once of Bekhor Ibrahim dressed in this way but it was lost along with our possessions during our exodus from Egypt.

My grandfather died young, leaving my great-grandmother with fourteen children to raise. My father said that he had made provisions for his family. They never wanted for anything. My father, the eldest, took responsibility as man of the family, investing in land and living off the rents. His family was rather haughty, and when he married they expected my mother to be docile and obedient, to be submissive to them. When I was indignant about the way they treated Mother, all Father said was, "*da tabee'i*" (that's natural). I didn't agree, and it upset me.

On Saturday mornings, my father's entire clan walked to the Moharram Bey synagogue, then came for breakfast at our house, where Mother never failed to lay a sumptuous table and where the servants were instructed to be extra vigilant in order to please the "master of the house." Mother rarely relaxed her own attentions enough to enjoy the meal or the conversation. She pressed everyone to eat "just a little bit more" and made sure glasses and plates were full, coaxing this uncle to try one dish and that aunt to try another. She evidently expected nothing more than this from her interactions with Father's family and Father expected nothing less. They both understood this was how things were. Mother's strategy was to maintain peace, but there was no spontaneity or genuine warmth expressed toward

Father's brothers and sisters or their families. She was deferential to them and somehow this pleased him. He could then boast about his dutiful and beautiful wife. She fulfilled her obligations and maintained the sacred Saturday rituals and those breakfasts, which I came to dread.

"Why do you do this for them week after week?" I asked.

She replied, "Vida, Daddy would be very upset if I didn't attend to his brothers and sisters in this way. You don't understand now, but one day you will." I never did, and when I married, I made sure from the start to set my own rules. But, of course, times and circumstances had changed by then. I created my own rules and obligations.

With her family, and especially with her sisters, Mother was a different person entirely than she was around Father's family. She was fun loving and full of humor. She smiled and laughed easily. With them, she escaped to the huge marble-floored bathroom on the second floor and locked the door when she could. It was a refuge where the sisters gossiped and giggled like girls. It was one place they knew they could not be overheard, especially by their husbands.

One day, Mother caught me listening at the door. She did not chastise me. Rather, she patted my head and said, "'nfish albi" [sic] (I was flushing out my heart).[4] What were they talking about? I'll never know, but I can tell you that when they came out of that bathroom they had mischief in their eyes.

There were two particularly prominent families in the Alexandria of my time: the Menasces and the Aghions; both were philanthropists. The Menasces built a girls' school and the Aghions a boys' school. The girls learned fine sewing and embroidery. The school eventually became an atelier that catered to upper-class Jews, Christians, and Muslims. They took orders for bridal trousseaux, sewing and embroidering fine lingerie, table linens, and bed linens, all of it done by hand. Most of the women who taught the girls at the school had been themselves taught by nuns, who had been taught by other nuns, who had come with Napoleon's expedition to Egypt. Orders abounded and had to be placed months in advance, with the exception of orders from members of the royal family. In my time, Safinaz Zulfiqar was a client. She became Queen Farida when she married King Faruq. Much later, another client was Nariman, Faruq's last wife, who went into exile with him and died in exile in 2005. Safinaz died in Maadi in 1988, I was told. The Atelier saw to the needs of hundreds of brides, but who knows what became of it after the Jews were expelled from Egypt!

My mother, Ariella Aharon, was not a member of the most elite of the Jewish families of Alexandria, but the family was well regarded and one of her brothers was a big shot in the Alexandrian Jewish community. She came from a family of five brothers and five sisters who were as vivacious as they were good looking. When they got together they laughed a lot and they liked to tell stories. My mother's signature story was about Aharon, who gave his name to the family. She recounted how Aharon and his brother Moshe met and confronted the Pharaoh in Egypt, asking that the Jews be released from bondage.

"Moshe and Aharon," Mother recounted, "held the destiny of the Jewish people in their hands. Aharon was the spokesman and he said to Pharaoh, 'Let my people go.' Instead, Pharaoh punished the Jews."

On cue, Aunt Serach interjected: "Yes, Ariella, but God brought plagues down on Egypt to punish Pharaoh for his cruelty, and eventually the Jews escaped."

This story was long and winding, and circulated in many forms in Mother's family as I was growing up.

My mother's sisters were delightful, but my father's sisters were a humorless lot who made it their business to find fault with my mother as often as they could. She was old-fashioned and had too many children, they said. She breastfed them too long, they said. She and her sisters wasted time telling stories, they said. And on and on. I dreaded Saturdays when they came. Father said they meant no harm. Mother bit her tongue, although on occasion she came out with a subtle retort.

"Don't you know that the Shulkhan Arukh says a woman should breast-feed for two to five years, Adina?" she told one of Father's sisters.

Another time, when Aunt Esther said that Moses had been breastfed by an Egyptian wet nurse, Mother replied, "He refused to nurse, Esther. He only took the tit from Yocheved, his own mother, who saved him when she placed him in a basket made of reeds to be found floating in the Nile by Pharaoh's daughter."

Before my mother married, she and her friends decided they wanted to do something for the Jewish community, not just sit around. They admired Florence Nightingale and so, in an effort to emulate her, they volunteered at the Jewish Hospital in Moharram Bey. They learned to care for the sick and to give injections, but once they married they had to give up this work. It was there that Father first saw Mother and said that he instantly fell in love with her. She really was beautiful, with her perfect skin, dark-gold hair, and blue eyes.

My father went to her father and asked for her hand in marriage. Of course, everyone knew everyone then. Everyone knew who were the marriageable girls and who were the young men looking for brides. Also, everyone knew which families were compatible, which suitors were suitable.

My mother's brothers did not think much of my father because he had the reputation of being a womanizer and also lived off his rents, not his labors. He did not earn a living, they explained, but collected rents from people who worked his agricultural lands. Despite the fact that he was rich, handsome, and cut quite a figure driving his horse-drawn phaeton, my mother's brothers objected to his lifestyle. In French, which they spoke fluently, they declared, "*C'est un rentier!*" They believed in 'work,' as in going to work daily, not living on the backs of others. My uncles flung out the word *rentier* like an insult and spoke disparagingly of members of this leisure class. Indeed, my father owned land and rented it to peasants who worked it, giving him a portion of the profits they made at harvest time. The better part went to the landowner. It was an unfair system, which exploited the poor, my uncles repeated. They wanted a steady, working man for their sister.

My uncles themselves owned businesses they had built from the ground up. They went to work daily, demonstrating a strong work ethic they wished to see in the man their sister married. Thus, when Father first presented himself, he was refused. Father would not back down, however, and my uncles, unable to ignore his persistence and the fact that their sister was drawn to him, threw him a bone, saying, "Go to work and promise never to look at another woman; then we can talk."

Father went into banking, determined to succeed as a "working man" and to prove himself worthy of Vida. I do think my mother was in love with him. She overlooked his imperiousness, which in my mind was one of his flaws. Could she have interpreted it as a form of manliness? As for his difficult family, she made accommodations. She really gave him her complete devotion along with her hand, offering daily her unflinching support and steady guidance until the day he died.

My mother raised us with the idea that education was of the utmost importance. We were all sent to school, boys and girls. The boys went to Ecole de Sainte Catherine, run by priests and nuns. Contrary to what you may think today, at that time it was believed that French was the most useful language for boys to learn to prepare them for life in business or commerce. English was best suited to a girl's life needs. To this end, my sisters and I were sent to the Scottish School, where our mother had also been a student. It was then located at Place Mohammad Ali, not far from the Temple Menasce, a beautiful synagogue in midtown Alexandria. Later, the school was moved to Chatby. When my sisters and I were old enough to go to school alone, we rode the streetcars and got off at the same stop as the students attending the Lycée Français. Eventually, my parents decided to send me to the Lycée, where I obtained my baccalaureate and graduated. Thus, I am at ease in English and in French.

At the Scottish School we were expected to recite prayers every morning. My sisters and I learned "Our father who art in heaven . . . " and so on. We even went to church sometimes. Mother did not object, saying that being exposed to other faiths and other cultures would expand our horizons.

All of us did well in school. Additionally, we had tutors at home. Mother hired a sheikh (Muslim cleric) to teach us Arabic and a rabbi to teach us Hebrew. The girls were also trained in the domestic arts and handiwork, fine sewing and embroidery. I was a bit of a tomboy and I sometimes escaped to join in games and sports with my brothers instead. As I also loved dance, Mother sent me to Madame Simanovska's studio in Mazarita for ballet lessons. She also helped me to join the Girl Guides and encouraged the ideas and activities promoted by them, as she believed they would contribute to my self-confidence, leadership skills, and independent spirit. My mother understood me and, having been raised in the Scottish School herself, she approved of the ethics and activities taught there. They certainly mirrored those of the Girl Guides. I think she thought the Guides would provide a good venue for me, a good place to expend my excess energy. She called me her "little firecracker," and said that she wished my brothers would join the Boy Scouts too, as it was an organization that promoted the social and physical wellbeing of youth. Mother was really an Anglophile. My brothers refused to join, however, saying, "The Boy Scouts are all for Arab nationalism and there is no place in that organization for Jewish boys." They joined the Maccabi instead, a Jewish scouting movement.

My brothers and I were physically active, and scouting further encouraged us. I was considered a bit of a tomboy and 'active' was my middle name—still is! Playing with my brothers, I had the upper hand as I could taunt and tease them, knowing they were not allowed to push back because I was a girl. Some of my pranks included climbing on top of armoires or bookcases and jumping out to surprise them, or even down on top of them. Hiding inside, I frustrated my brothers, who knew I was hiding, and could guess where, but knew they were neither allowed to pull me out of a wardrobe I was pretending was my cave, nor yank me off a bookcase from which I attacked them, laughing and screeching with delight. I had the best of two worlds: my brothers' world of play and the world of dolls and typically feminine activities.

I still remember my favorite doll. Her name was Couchette, and she was a curly-haired blonde just like me. She was my pride and joy, but I did not grieve long for her when she broke. I took a lot for granted then, but could also have just been more interested in boyish activities, preferring my brothers' company to giving tea parties for dolls.

In my day, it was not unusual for children to learn several languages at once. We spoke French, especially with my brothers. I spoke English with my sisters, Italian with the maids, and sometimes all three languages with Mother. Children from families like ours rarely spoke Arabic, calling it the "language of the servants." What did we know? Our parents, however, insisted we learn it and reminded us that our ancestor Bekhor Ibrahim, who prospered in Egypt, did so in part because he spoke it fluently. Father told the boys that Arabic would be an asset and would serve them well when negotiating in the Middle East and even in the Arab world. How stupid and narrow-minded so many of us were who despised this beautiful language!

Mother raised us with the idea that nothing we wanted to do was impossible. I liked art and so I was given painting lessons by an Armenian painter named Zoyan. I was very good and at the end of my first year of training I exhibited and was admitted to the Ecole des Beaux Arts, located across from the Sidi Metwally Mosque, steps from Mahattat Masr (Cairo Station) in Alexandria. When I showed my work at our final exhibition just before graduation, I was awarded first prize, which qualified me for a government scholarship to study in Paris. These were called 'Missions.' Upon earning a degree abroad, students were expected to return to Egypt and teach in the public schools for a minimum of two years. I was sixteen and couldn't wait to get to Paris. My parents said I was too young to set out on my own and refused to let me go. Nothing I said could persuade them otherwise. I was crushed as I watched the second-prize winner, a Coptic girl, go in my place. Interestingly, when I met her again, she said to me, "*Ya bakhtik, tu es mariée et tu a des enfants!*" (Lucky you, you are married and have children!) Evidently, she was wedded to art and never married or enjoyed motherhood. It was a different world then. Today, women can have many strings to their bows, as the old saying goes. We have come a long way!

My father died at age fifty-four of a heart attack, and my brothers took up where he left off. All of his life, my father suffered from hemorrhoids and they may have killed him. In the 1930s there was no surgery for them. It was only when Professor Crecenski came to Egypt and opened the Italian Hospital near the Rondpoint in the Greek quarter that such surgeries were introduced. Still, they were risky and, in my father's case, deadly. The day of his surgery, Father hemorrhaged and the nuns rushed him into the operating room. The operation was performed without anesthetic and he suffered terribly. The next day, when we came to see him, he was utterly devastated. He said to me, "My heart raced right out of my body. The nuns and the surgeons were there, but I felt abandoned, Vida. I was terrified!" Digitaline was prescribed. He took it, lived another two years, and died suddenly. I think the shock of this experience affected his heart and caused his untimely death our last summer together at Abukir.

Many Jewish families summered in Abukir and many also went to Ras al-Barr. Whereas at Abukir the water of the Mediterranean was bright blue, at Ras al-Barr the water was brown. You could see the Delta; you could see clearly just where the Nile met the Mediterranean. Three months of each summer, life flowed easily and we lived carefree as gypsies in huts at Abukir. They were called *'eshash* and were about a hundred square feet total, with partitions for rooms and a kitchen area outside. In the summer of 1933, Father purchased a REO Royale Sedan and one of my brothers drove us to the train station in it. There was excellent service between Alexandria and Abukir and no one ever thought of driving there. At Abukir we were met by donkey carts, which carried us to our camps. We either cooked in camp or went to Hotel Shemol, which was owned by a Jewish family who ran a kosher restaurant.

Father was already quite ill that summer and told me he wanted me at his side. I was the closest of the children to him. He wanted me and Mother near him and would not let us out of his sight. We took care of him with the help of our maid and loved every moment we saw him enjoying Abukir, sensing it could be his last season there. My sister Bella came to visit, too. Her husband, a Greek physician, raised concern when he saw Daddy, saying he did not look well. Had we considered going back to Alexandria a little early this year? We had not, but did, and in the first week of September Daddy had a massive heart attack and was gone instantly. Bella died at twenty-six, two years later, on the very same day as Father. Mother was inconsolable. She dressed in mourning and remained dressed in black the rest of her life. Amazingly, Mother too died on the same day as Father and Bella.

Bella's story is interesting. Over Mother's objections, she moved to Sudan with her husband. In Khartoum, she caught a deadly fever, which killed her. Mother was never the same after this. My brothers took over Father's business and I took over running the household. I was responsible for creating menus for the cook, directing the maids and the gardener, and so on. Because Father, Mother, and Bella died on the same day, I hold joint memorial services for them until this day.

My brother married a woman from a wealthy Jewish family with prosperous businesses in the Orient. He met her while on business and they took to each other instantly. Her father, seeing this, proposed to Felix that he marry Izabel and join the family business and eventually take it over. My brother accepted. They were traveling on board ship to Alexandria to meet us. The ship caught fire during the crossing and caused the death of a number of passengers, including Izabel's mother. When they finally arrived in Alexandria, my brother urged me to take care of his fiancée, to try help her recover from the shock of her loss.

Felix said, "See what you can do to boost Iza's morale, Vida. She is not just sick with grief, but sick with the shock the accident has caused her body." She had jumped from the burning ship and swallowed a lot of salt water before being rescued.

All of my life the family turned to me in times of stress, counting on my strength and resilience to help everyone through. I told Felix I would look after Iza, and immediately took her under my wing and with me on all of my outings. Despite the loss of her mother, Izabel decided to marry Felix in Egypt and return to Singapore a few months later. She and I had grown fond of each other and she invited me to travel back with them. I was reluctant to leave Mother, but so eager for adventure that I did not hesitate to accept Iza's invitation. I agreed to go and went about having fourteen evening gowns made for the occasion.

As I said, life was easy and pleasant, and we just enjoyed ourselves so much. We traveled first class on board a ship belonging to the P&O lines and our first port of call was Bombay. We sailed twenty-one days, then went on to Aden, to Ceylon, and finally to Singapore, where I left Felix and Iza to adjust to their new lives and went off on my own as a tourist. I was only twenty-two, but I was fearless and loved this newfound independence. I had a wonderful time seeing new places, and meeting boys who wanted to marry me. I was a pretty girl then. I admit, I flirted, but refused them all. My future bridegroom was waiting for me in Alexandria, though I did not know it at the time.

This trip to accompany Felix and Iza gave me a taste for travel, and I subsequently went to visit family in Europe. I even took classes at the Sorbonne and La Grande Chaumière. I relished these moments of freedom as, having become a sort of mother figure in my family, they were rare. It was one of the reasons I married late. I made myself available to my family. If anyone needed anything, it was Vida do this and Vida do that, Vida can you come, Vida can you stay, and so on. Some appreciated my attention and care; others resented it. Interesting, don't you think? There is truth in the Jewish proverb that says to beware those to whom you have done a kindness. Anyway, my brothers had friends looking for marriageable girls and they introduced me, but none ever seemed right to me.

The year I turned twenty-five, however, Aaron, who was thirty, caught my eye and it seems he noticed me as well. He had family in the United States and it was this family who sheltered us when we were expelled from Egypt. Aaron was unassuming and relaxed, and said he had never met anyone he wanted to marry before me. I was the same. He courted me, won me over with his good humor, and a year later we married. He was a very warm, kind man, and these qualities appealed to me. I think my strength appealed to him. We had two boys together and thought we would spend the rest of our lives in Egypt, but, as you can see, that was not to be.

I do not want to remember our terrible last moments in Egypt and so I will not speak of them. Suffice to say that we were ousted, and left for the United States with one suitcase, the clothes on our backs, and a couple hundred dollars. Once there, I organized my work and my life, saying, "I'm never going to go back even if I can," and family members who did, years later, said to me, "If you want to remember the Egypt you left, then don't return. Your heart will break!"

My last memory of Egypt was the Chatby cemetery, where I went before our sad departure to pay respects to my family members buried there. I went to say a final goodbye, sure I would never return. As you will see, destiny had other plans.

When rumors reached me in New York, just a year before my eightieth birthday, that the Chatby cemetery was now taken over by the city and falling into disrepair, I wondered how I could overcome my dread of returning to Egypt and go see what I could do to help.

My last remaining sibling, my brother Sam, had never left Egypt. He had met a Muslim woman, a member of the royal family of Egypt, and fallen in love with Malika. He converted to Islam and they married and lived together thirty some years until she died a couple of years before my return to Egypt. I knew I would be in good hands if I decided to go back for one last visit. I thought about it, then pushed the idea right out of my mind. What was I thinking!

The reports about Chatby kept troubling me and the rumors that our burial grounds were on the verge of desecration shattered me. The government, rumor had it, wanted to unearth the bones of the Jewish dead and give them to their families, or put them somewhere else.

Finally, I contacted Sam, who said, "It's only a rumor, Vida, but you never know what can happen in Egypt. *Ihna a'deen 'ala kaff 'afreet*, we are sitting in the palm of a devil who delights in harming us and shows no mercy."

One day, in passing, I mentioned my conversation with Sam to my boys, adding, "How I wish I could do something about Chatby!" I left it at that. It was in January of 1995. We had been gone from Egypt for nearly fifty years.

When March came around, and with it my birthday on the thirtieth, the boys came to see me and said, "We have a surprise for you, Mother. You are going to spend your eightieth birthday in Egypt."

I protested. "Absolutely not! I don't want to go to Egypt. I don't want to go back, birthday or no birthday."

They said, "Mother, we have bought the tickets and they are non-refundable."

Cheap as I am, the argument persuaded me, although I tried a last time to ask them to see if they could return the tickets.

"Find a way," I pleaded, although in my heart of hearts I knew this was my wish come true. Beware what you wish for!

So, with my TWA roundtrip ticket in hand, I began preparations. I renewed my passport and called my brother, who was thrilled to have me come.

"I'll make all the arrangements and I'll be expecting her," Sam said to my sons.

They were thrilled to know their gift was precious to me, despite my protestations.

"I'll be waiting at Cairo Airport for her and drive her directly back to Alexandria, show her around for a few days, and then surprise her with a Nile cruise," Sam told them. "Vida will love it!"

My boys said, "Uncle Samuel has arranged everything. It will be the trip of a lifetime, Mother. You will love it!"

Before I knew it, I was on Trans World Airlines, flying from New York to Cairo. The stewardesses were very solicitous as I was traveling alone. One of them was quite chatty and asked about me and my family.

I said, "I grew up in Egypt and am returning to see my brother and to celebrate my eightieth birthday. This trip is a gift from my sons."

"Oh, my goodness," she said. "Traveling alone for your birthday! You don't look a day over sixty!"

Of course, I was pleased. And more so when a few minutes later I heard my name announced on the loudspeaker: "We have a very special passenger on our flight to Cairo today. Her name is Vida. She is returning to Egypt to celebrate her eightieth birthday. We all want to wish her a very happy birthday."

Before you knew it, the whole plane was looking at me and singing "Happy birthday to you, happy birthday to you." The stewardess offered me a bottle of champagne, which I put in my carry-on to enjoy after landing. It was called Mum Red, one of the best champagnes. I was so touched by the attention and their gesture that I wrote their names in calligraphy during the course of the eleven-hour flight and gave them each a card I had previously hand decorated. They oohed and aahed, and kissed me goodbye when we landed. Despite the arduous trip, I disembarked feeling refreshed and elated. I was in seventh heaven with my bottle of champagne tucked into my *fourre-tout* (holdall) in one hand and my pocketbook in the other. We arrived into Cairo at two o'clock in the afternoon and were met with a blast of heat. I remembered March in Egypt with its hot winds off the desert and the red sand that crept into every crevice. For a moment, but only really for a moment, I thought, "I am home."

Sam was waiting for me with his chauffeur-driven Mercedes, a beautiful cream-colored antique. He looked so old, and this was a shock. You remember people as you last saw them, of course. No doubt he thought the same about me but, ever the gentleman, said, "*Tu as l'air magnifique!*" (You look magnificent!)

I got a fancy new haircut before leaving, at an expensive salon because I had done some work for the owner. One of my friends had called me, saying, "Vida, I have a job for you. So-and-so is having an exhibit of handmade jewelry and he wants you to pen the invitations for him. He will pay you." The "so-and-so" was the owner of a high-end hairstyling salon, who was so pleased with my work that he offered me a free haircut.

He said, "Come in on the Monday before your trip," which I did, and he gave me the best haircut of my life, saying, "You are a beautiful woman and you have beautiful eyes and you make them up so nicely . . ." and words of this nature. Of course, an octogenarian loves to hear such compliments. And, when my brother saw me and said, "You look fantastic," I was in seventh heaven.

My first emotion was joy at seeing my brother. On the drive back to Alexandria, we chatted. We had a lot of catching up to do. He took the desert road, which I did not recognize at all as it was now cultivated and had buildings all along the way. We did stop at the old Rest House, which had been owned by Greeks when we were growing up. It was the same, though much busier.

I said to my brother, "This is not the desert route . . ."

He answered, "*Oui, c'est la même route* (Yes, it's the same route), but it has changed so much. There is so much change, Vida, that you will be surprised. Wait and see."

I was not only surprised, but amazed, in fact aghast!

I commented about the greening of the desert: "They are trying to imitate what is going on in Israel."

Sam agreed.

Finally, we got home. And where was home? A beautiful villa on the beach, in Agami.

Agami, which used to be a quiet, deserted place with nothing but a few cabins on the Mediterranean, had become a city. The big thing was that

King Faruq's second wife, Nariman, had built a villa there, at which point Agami became all the rage.

I said, "This can't be Agami!" But it was. I couldn't believe how built-up it was, couldn't believe all the houses, post office, banks, stores, pharmacies, the crowding.

"This isn't the end of it," my brother said. "What you are going to see around you is going to absolutely amaze you."

I said, "It looks so dirty and crowded. This is not the Egypt I remember!"

He said, "I can imagine. Now, it's elbow-to-elbow people and the congestion on the roads and the traffic jams are terrible. If you want to remember Alexandria or even Agami as they were, forget it Vida. Think of them as two new cities you have never visited before and you won't be disappointed."

He was right. When we went to Alexandria, I did not recognize a single apartment building, any of the streets, not even the neighborhood where we used to live in our beautiful twenty-two-room mansion in the Greek quarter.

When we were expelled, we gave the chauffeur our villa, and when I saw it, I was shocked. My heart sank. I didn't even want to stop and look in. It had not been painted in forty years and everything was falling apart, including the garden, which was now all weeds. I wept. I didn't want to see any more. I couldn't believe that where we grew up in such wealth and such prosperity had come to this: decrepitude!

When Sam saw the tears rolling down my cheeks, he said, "Forget the Egypt you knew, Vida. This is what has happened."

My brother's villa in Agami was lovely despite the general deterioration surrounding it. He and Malika had built it on two acres of land and had designed the gardens together, adding rooms, a kitchen, and a bathroom for servants at the far end of the property. A stand of casuarina trees was planted to shield the servants' quarters from the rest of the property.

In conversation one evening, I asked Sam if he would ever consider moving to be closer to family now that Malika had passed. He said, "I can't take any of my assets out of the country. Besides, I'm used to my life here and I wouldn't want to change."

My brother lives well in Egypt and so I understand why he would not want to change that. He could never live as comfortably elsewhere at this time in his life. He has a housekeeper from Sri Lanka, a boy to clean the house, two gardeners, a chauffeur, and two cooks.

I said to him, "Why two cooks, Sam?"

He answered, "Don't ask questions, Vida. Just live and see."

So I did. The reason he had those two cooks soon became clear. His was an open house, with people dropping in daily to socialize, eat, drink, and, as I discovered to my surprise, smoke *sheesha* (water pipes). His friends were mostly Egyptian, some were Muslim, some Coptic, with a smattering of European expatriates, and a few liberal Jews from a community that had now shrunk to almost nothing. There were not quite a hundred in all of Egypt when I visited. Despite his having converted, my brother still contributes time and money to maintaining the synagogue and the cemeteries.

After I had rested a couple of days, my brother said, "Now, I'm going to take you around and I'm going to take you to the cemetery. This is what you want to see."

I discovered that the cemetery in Alexandria was still beautiful. It was the only landmark I could have recognized. When word was sent that I would visit, the gardener put in beautiful fresh flowers. I took a huge bouquet and cried my eyes out. My parents and my twenty-six-year-old sister, my family, had all lain buried there for nearly a century. My brother told me he had heard nothing about exhuming the bones. It may have been a different matter in Cairo. There, the cemeteries were crumbling and vandalized. I had no one there to visit and did not ask to go. I visited the cemetery in Alexandria, took photos, and by the end of the day was utterly spent, emotionally drained. I rested for the remainder of that day.

When evening came, I freshened up and joined the company. The maid and cooks had set a big round table laden with food. There were three or four kinds of cold cuts and cheeses, and *dukka*, a kind of sprinkling mix made with sesame seeds, a very Jewish thing. There was also hot food.

I asked my brother, "What happens in the evening?"

He said, "Wait and you will see." So I did.

People came all evening and the telephone did not stop ringing. About eight o'clock everyone served themselves buffet style, and Sam explained, "That's what we do every night for dinner."

I watched his friends loading their plates. I was not used to this volume of food and ate very little, but enjoyed it and went to bed early. I was jet-lagged; it had been a long trip, and the cemetery had also taken a lot out of me. The maid followed me into the bedroom with a glass of warm milk and asked what time I wanted to get up. I usually got up at seven, but I thought

I would sleep a little later, until eight or nine. As soon as she left, I got ready for bed. I lay down and slept like a log.

A knock at my door in the morning woke me. I was groggy and a bit confused, and croaked, "Who is it?"

The maid answered, "*al-hammam be-yestannaki*" (a bath awaits you).

In Egypt, somebody heats the bathwater for you and prepares the bath. It was a luxury I had forgotten.

Sam said to me when we arrived in Agami: "Vida, get used to it. You are going to be a lady for as long as you are here." And so I was.

He added, "The way you live in New York . . . goodness! You have to shop, cook, clean, and all this, and you tell me you don't wish to live anywhere else? I don't understand you after the life you lived in Egypt!"

Growing up, we had maids preparing baths and making breakfast any time you got up. Now the maid brought me coffee, toast, butter and jam, yogurt and fruit, and I asked her, "Did you buy all this?"

She said, "Oh, no, no, lady, everything is homemade!"

After breakfast my brother took me around Alexandria. He warned, "Don't be disappointed. Possibly the only place that has not changed since you left is Muntazah." Muntazah was where King Faruq summered and where he married his second wife, Nariman. I found it exactly as it used to be.

One place I visited had actually improved, and that was the Greco-Roman Museum near my brother's clinic. I had expressed a desire to visit the museum, remembering it as a dusty little place with little to distinguish it. He said nothing about the renovations there, probably allowing for the pleasure of a surprise. He sent a woman who worked with him to accompany me, saying it was only to make sure I didn't get lost.

He said, "I'm going to the clinic and Salma is going to go with you. It's better this way."

So, Salma came and paid the entrance fees: fifty piasters (about thirty cents) for herself and eight pounds for me. The exchange rate was three pounds to the dollar at that time. I questioned her about the disparity in the price of the tickets, saying in Arabic, "*Leh ba'a?*" (Why is this?)

She said, "*Alashan ana masriya we-inti agnabiya.*" (Because I am Egyptian and you are a foreigner.) It sounded very strange to me.

Another thing I found strange was that all the female museum employees were dressed in the Tarha, the scarf around the head, and wore no makeup at all. This was the trend even for little girls going to school. As for the museum, they have enlarged it and cleaned it, and it is more beautiful than it ever was.

In New York, I belong to the Metropolitan Museum and so I had a few questions to ask and requested a meeting with the director.

Salma said, "Why do you ask for the director? They never want to talk to anyone."

I insisted, saying, "Why not?" So she asked the guard, who answered loudly, "Talk to the director! Why does she want to talk to the director?"

I surprised him by answering in Arabic, saying, "Oh, it's just to ask a few questions."

As we spoke, a lady came out and asked, "*Eh, eh, fee eh, ya Hamed?*" (What's wrong, Hamed?)

He said, "*La' mafeesh haga, ya Mudira. El-sitt di 'ayzat shufik, ya Madam.*" (No, there's nothing wrong, Director. It's just that this lady wants to see you, Ma'am.)

"Come in," she said. "Welcome."

I said, "My Arabic is not that good. Is it possible to speak to you in English?"

She took me into her office, to the amazement of Salma and the guard, invited me to sit down, and offered me a cup of coffee. I told her about my membership at the Metropolitan and asked her about the Greco-Roman, saying how much better it looked than when I was young. Just as she was explaining, another lady came in speaking French. She had just written a book about the museum and was going to have it published. We talked a little in English, a little in French, with a smattering of Arabic, just as we used to do in Egypt in the old days. For about thirty minutes they gave me a lot of information about how they cleaned up the museum and reorganized it, then took me to see the exquisite Tanagras just as a group of schoolchildren came through on a field trip. Otherwise, the museum was empty.

At the time I came to Egypt, people were afraid of going to the Middle East. I found this out on the cruise my brother had planned. Funny though, I felt much more secure in Egypt than I do in the States. When I mentioned this feeling to Sam, he said, "The only reason I want you to be with somebody is because I'm afraid you might get lost; that's all. I'm not worried about your safety. Security here is much, much better than it is in the States because punishment is greater, so people think twice before acting out of turn."

I spent a long time at the museum because I enjoyed it so much. I went to the gift shop next, which carried Egyptian artifacts and folk art. At first I was crazy and wanted to buy everything.

Salma insisted, "*La' ya Madam, da ghali awi, ana hashtereelik haga ma'ula*" (No, Madam, this is too expensive, I'll get it for you at a more reasonable price).

She then took my shopping list and I went back to my brother's clinic. She paid two pounds for trinkets I was going to pay fifteen for. I waited for an hour or so at the clinic while my brother took care of one or two patients. He gave me something to read, and I had another cup of Turkish coffee, which I love, and a glass of water perfumed with rose essence. It brought back memories. My brother, when he was done, then took me around some more and we went home. In the evening company came again and it was full of conversation and laughter. Anyone could drop in, have a drink, eat, and smoke a *sheesha*. Sam was a generous and genial host and he loved having people around him.

I was surprised at seeing *sheesha* though, which I associated with native coffeehouses in popular neighborhoods. Yet, here it was at my brother's elegant villa.

I said, "Since when have you used the *sheesha*?"

He just said, "I love the *sheesha*!"

Evidently, my brother had adopted everything Egyptian and wherever we went people greeted him, "*Ya basha, ya duktur . . .*" He was loved.

The following day I had to go to the bank to exchange traveler's checks.

My brother said, "I don't know if the bank in Agami can do this. You may have to go to Alexandria, but let's go and see."

We had breakfast and then went to the bank and it was absolutely packed. Time means nothing there. People wait patiently for a bus, for help, for everything. At the bank, someone said, "There is going to be a long wait." However, not two minutes later, the manager called out to my brother: "*Ahlan, ya Doctor, ahlan wa sahlan, izzayak ya Doctor*," words of greeting and welcome. He took us right into his office. In fifteen minutes the transaction was complete and we had been offered mint tea while a junior clerk did the legwork.

I said, "It's not fair to the other people waiting!"

Sam answered, "Don't ask for fairness here, Vida. Take advantage of what is offered and enjoy it."

One thing that drove me nuts was the way people wove in and out of traffic. No one paid attention to traffic lights, green lights, red lights—everyone did as they pleased. You had to be a wizard to cross any street and to drive without accident.

My brother said, "That's just how it is. No discipline." It's odd to me, but he seems to actually enjoy the energy in all that chaos.

My brother's wife was a Muslim, as I said. His marrying her surprised no one as they had been together for years. Our parents were dead and there really was no one to object to his converting to Islam to marry Malika. Sam said, and Malika believed, it was a mere formality.

When trouble started with Nasser, none of us had Egyptian citizenship. We had French passports. We were expelled, but my brother was protected by his marriage to Malika, who nevertheless gave him the keys to the family home at the 'izba (farm) and said to stay there until things calmed down. She was a member of the royal family and the revolutionaries did not hurt the royal family, whom they treated with consideration even as they toppled their dynasty. She took care of Sam and made sure he was safe.

One of my brothers living in United States worked as an emergency-room doctor at Harlem Hospital. He told Sam how rugged things were, what with the stabbings, the heat in summer, and so on. In a letter, which I have, he wrote: "If you can do it, stay in Egypt." Even if Sam had considered leaving, he saw that it would be impossible to get his money out. Also, he had a lot of beautiful stuff and he couldn't give me even one of his antiques, saying, "Everything is catalogued by the government. I can't get rid of anything without telling them." I think Sam is really most comfortable where he is, even with Malika now gone.

I said to him one morning, "To think that at your age you still have to work!"

He said, "But I like it, don't you see?"

It is a bittersweet feeling I had upon setting foot in Egypt again. I was very happy to see my brother, but disappointed by how changed it was. The Nile cruise Sam took me on was wonderful, however. Also, I enjoyed the Egyptian Museum in Cairo. He and I visited the museum, then flew to Aswan, boarded a ship, and sailed to Luxor. Wonderful!

Before leaving he had arranged for a cake and a birthday celebration. There was champagne and grape leaves and tahini and all the things I like to eat, and we talked and talked and talked. At one point, after asking about this person and that one, he finally said, "*Ecoute, ne commence pas par m'ennuyer* (stop bothering me), everybody is dead!" So, I focused on the party, which was on Saturday night, and had a wonderful time. Sunday he made me a "Foulade" for brunch. That is *fuul medammes* (Egyptian fava beans, the national dish) served with eggs, olives, tomatoes, feta cheese, pita bread, the works! All the time people came and went, and I don't know how I kept up the pace but I did. I read for an hour or so while resting in between events and visits, and always stayed dressed until evening, when I undressed to go to bed.

My brother kept saying, "I am doing this for my old sister," but nobody believed I was eighty.

Finally, we left for the cruise aboard a Presidential Line ship. Coincidentally, the owner of these Nile ships was the son of the owner of the hotel where I had stayed in Luxor on my honeymoon. On board, I had a room by myself and Sam another. I had packed skirts and tops that could drip dry and a very nice heavy sweater and a lighter jacket. I had three skirts—black, brown, navy, and off-white—and blouses to match. During the day I dressed casually, washed and dried my things in the bathroom, and kept clothes folded on the second bunk as I couldn't reach up to hang them in the closet because of my frozen shoulder. It was March and still cold, so I slept wrapped in my sweater and an extra blanket. There was no central heating.

There were young Egyptians on board and I told them about when Tut's tomb was discovered and how King Fuad opened it especially for groups of students who went down to see it with torches. I was among them. King Fuad wanted young people to get to know their heritage and had said, "I want the young ones who are going to be the older ones to know enough to talk about Egypt to their children." Our parents had not told most of us about Upper Egypt and it was not until these school trips that we had any inkling of its history, its magnificence.

King Fuad was there when I went to Luxor with my school group. I will never forget that encounter. He had reserved fixed train cars by the hundreds, sixteen berths in each car for schoolchildren; eight for girls and eight for boys on each trip. He sent children for the equivalent of $5 per child to Luxor, and if you had no money, you went for free. I went with a group of girls from the Lycée Français. It was summer. We traveled by night, and in the morning came out of the train and there were leaders and monitors waiting to take us to a kind of open-air place for breakfast. It was a tent erected specially for us near the train station. This is where we had all of our meals. They were tasty but basic. We had ful in the morning, bread and cheese for lunch, and soup for dinner. You could have as much bread as you wanted at any meal. The train was our hotel. It was hot at this time of the year, but beautiful. There were very few bathrooms, but we made do. We were instructed to stay with our school group at all times, and not to mix with others. The teachers and monitors were strict but we had a ball. Most of the time we were out, visiting sites. When I went, Tut's tomb was the newest site and our group was among the first to see it in 1923. We went down with torches and it was dark and mysterious, romantic and fantastic. I enjoyed it so much and also enjoyed being with boys and girls my age. Of course the boys and girls slept in separate cars. My brother Felix was there, too. It was one of the nicest experiences I have ever had. I was in a group of eight girls and we laughed and joked from the moment we woke up, tickling each other, punching each other. It was such fun! In the morning we went to the bathrooms, cleaned up as best we could, dressed, and were led on our visits. Hundreds of children were given this opportunity. We were Jews, Muslims, Christians together, one big family.

The next time I went to Luxor was on my honeymoon. When a girl married in winter, she went to Upper Egypt. If a girl married in summer, she went to Europe. Honeymoons lasted a month or two. My new husband and I and stayed at the Luxor Hotel, which was one of the nicest hotels at that time. I remember being quiet and pensive, and not as excited about the trip as my bridegroom was hoping I would be. He made a remark and I said to him, "You know, it's wonderful being here, but if you knew what a lovely time we had for the $5 we paid when I was a schoolgirl, you would understand that nothing I do now can beat it." He was very upset and I said no more, although I wanted to share my schoolgirl experience with him. I loved my husband's company but didn't enjoy the two months we spent in Luxor half as much as I enjoyed the evenings and the days with my friends as a schoolgirl. That is the truth. I cannot hide it. I did love seeing Abu Simbel with Aaron, though, and visiting the Begum Agha Khan when we stayed at the Old Cataract in Aswan. She spoke fluent French and was always happy to welcome visitors in the afternoon.

I am glad I had a chance to go back to Egypt after all. It was, as my boys said it would be, the trip of a lifetime. We had been happy in Egypt and leaving was hard. But we adjust and move on and I see no need to dwell on the painful moments, or even to recount them. And so, the world turns, everything changes and we change too. Egypt remains etched in my mind as a new Egypt, but the memories of how it once was, how we lived there, is the more real of the two.

This, my dear, is my story of growing up in Egypt, revisiting Egypt and vowing never again to return. I've washed Egypt out of my hair, as Mary Martin sang in *South Pacific*. I choose to live in the here and now.

2
Adina

Meeting Adina

I met Adina at the Apthorp Apartments in Manhattan in 1987, shortly after meeting Vida. She lived in a large, elegant corner unit in this historic Italianate building on Broadway, where she had asked Vida to bring me to tea. She had heard about our encounter at the Brooklyn Museum and was eager to meet a "fellow Egyptian," as she put it.

One rainy spring afternoon, Vida and I walked through the massive wrought-iron doors leading to the enormous Apthorp courtyard, rushing past the round fountain spouting water around marble cherubs. It mimicked the heavy rain. Once in the building, we were met by a doorman who called Adina to verify our identities. We were ushered to an elevator. When Adina opened her door, the first thing she said was, "Spring is arriving in galoshes this year!" We laughed. This seemed like Egyptian humor, I thought, as I looked beyond Adina to the huge, high-ceilinged foyer, which reminded me of elegant apartments in Cairo and Alexandria. I wondered if it had appealed to her in part for this reason.

Adina stood tall, erect, smiling, a 'foxy' lady in her sixties. She had milk-white skin, and her face was lightly made up. She was dressed in a coral silk kaftan with buttons of the same hue, woven with silk thread and looking like tiny pearls. She fingered them often during our conversation and I wondered, "Do they have a message they wish to impart?" I suppressed a chuckle, but she noticed and smiled, saying, "My *sebha*, my prayer beads." It was more Egyptian-style humor. She made me feel immediately at ease.

Adina had impeccably manicured nails, painted pink. Did her toes match? I couldn't see them, as she had on a pair of high-heeled mules of the same silk as her kaftan, no doubt custom-made. Her hair, pulled back in a slick chignon, was a deep coral. Red from a bottle? I wondered. Her eyes, brown, lustrous, and slightly upturned under dark plucked eyebrows, were full of smiles as she served us tea from a silver service, offering baklava, tiny sandwiches, and berries.

The afternoon light seemed to leap into dusk as our visit drew to an end. Conversation was easy, and time flew. We covered a multitude of topics and Egypt was at the heart of each.

I felt that first day that Adina and I were destined to become friends. A year later, when she offered to let me tape-record her story, I was thrilled. Here it is.

Adina tells her story

My name is Adina Adler and I was born in the port city of Alexandria, to Austrian parents who left Europe before the Holocaust.

I am a professor of literature and came by my love of the written word early in life when I received a children's book of Ancient Egyptian stories from my grandmother on the occasion of my third birthday. I fell in love with the pictures of the gods and goddesses with their amazing animal heads and quickly learned to read so I could delve into their stories. I have not stopped reading since those long-ago days in Alexandria. In fact, I still have that first book of stories, which was one of the few items I packed and was able to take with me when we left Egypt forever. Today, I take equal pleasure in reading fiction, nonfiction, history, mythology, and poetry. I also enjoy studying world religions.

My parents and grandmother encouraged my passion for reading. Every Sunday morning one of them took me to Cité du Livre to browse the bookshelves and pick out a book to take home. I always relished the shelf of new arrivals and went there first to see if I could pick out from among them my book for the week. It became a tradition all the years I was growing up for my grandmother or parents to buy me a book, and by the time we left Egypt I had an extensive collection of children's books. Many I had to leave behind. I remember distinctly the Babar books. I loved them. In 1931, for my birthday, my grandmother bought me the first one, *L'Histoire de Babar, le petit éléphant*, and subsequently, I collected all of Jean de Brunhoff's books. Years later, I bought the English translations for my children as gifts. That is how much I loved these stories.

But I stray. Nessim Mustacchi, father of the famous singer Georges Moustaki, owned Cité du Livre, this downtown bookstore, which was a gathering place for young and old. It was located on Rue Fuad and held worlds and treasures on its creaking bookshelves. When I remember my expeditions to his bookstore and my first reading adventures, it is the smell of old paper and wood that comes to mind and takes me back to my childhood. To this day, when I first hold a book in my hands, I sniff it. I remember distinctly Mr. Mustacchi, his warm welcome and his enthusiastic readiness to recommend a book to young and old. I could not get enough of books back then, and today this is still true. As a child, I looked forward all week to Sunday mornings at the bookstore. It was my favorite activity.

I will tell you now about my family, which, like so many other Jewish families, came to Egypt for the rewarding and comfortable life it offered. The people were friendly, the climate was mild, and opportunities abounded.

Let me start with my father's mother, Dr. Margrete Edersheim Adler, Oma. She was born and raised in Vienna in the heart of a prosperous Ashkenazi family of entrepreneurs. She married young. My grandfather, Emil Adler, sadly passed away, leaving her a widow with a baby. My father, Albert, their only child, was born also in Vienna. Austrian Jews in the nineteenth century gave their children European instead of Hebrew names, hence Albert.

After my grandfather died and my grandmother had mourned for a year, she took charge of her life. She was, as I remember her, a take-charge kind of person. She decided she wanted to become a medical doctor, an unusual step for a woman in her social position at that time. But, being Margrete, she was not going to allow anything to get in the way of a dream. Furthermore, because she had resources, she had choices and the means to implement her dreams.

The story goes that Margrete applied to medical school in Switzerland and was accepted. To the chagrin of her family, however, she took Albert with her. She also took a nanny who would tend to him as she pursued her studies at the University of Zurich. After the requisite number of years, she graduated with a specialty in obstetrics and gynecology. Why did she do it? How did she do it? I had taken her for granted as I was growing up and it never occurred to me to ask her questions about her past or press her for information on her history. I looked for answers after she died, however. I went through her papers, diaries, and letters, hoping to understand her.

Her diaries were sparse and the letters were brief. But, tucked in among some papers, I found a sepia-toned photograph. I was able to identify Dr. Gabriele Possanner von Ehrenthal because of Oma's notation on the back. In her slanted handwriting, faded to a brown wash, I could make out "MD, Un. Zurich," but could not make out the date. My curiosity piqued, I determined to find out who this Dr. Gabriele might be. I discovered that she, like Oma, had graduated with a medical degree from the University of Zurich. Additionally, she had received a doctorate from the University of Vienna, and had gone on to become the only female doctor at an Austrian-Hungarian hospital before World War I. She served as a public medical officer and treated Muslim women in Bosnia-Herzegovina who couldn't see a male doctor. I wondered if Dr. Gabriele had been a role model for Margrete. In a flight of fancy, I imagined a meeting between them and wrote a story I entitled "Two Doctors." I intended to expand it, but it was lost in the shuffle of life. By the time I was settled enough to return to it, too much time had elapsed and there was no one left to talk to about Oma's intrepid move nor anyone who could add to the little I knew of my grandmother's early history. I suppose I could have attempted a work of fiction. I still might.

My mother, Lalita Landolfi, was born in Trieste, an important port city on the Adriatic Sea, ninety miles east of Venice. Before my parents left for Egypt, Trieste (once part of the Austro-Hungarian Empire) was a major trading port and shipbuilding center, seat of the Austrian Lloyd shipping lines, which owned and operated a fleet of cargo and passengers vessels traveling between Trieste and many port cities, including Alexandria. It was on board one of their ships—the *Thalia*, I think—that my parents, Oma, and my uncle Edgar made a journey that was to be the first step toward their Egyptian destinies. Let me explain about Uncle Edgar. Grandmother had taken this son of her husband's brother Jacob under her wing after his parents succumbed to smallpox, and he became part of their Egyptian migration, as did their maid, Elvira. Like so many other women in service, Elvira was from the village of Gorizia, which provided maids to European families and Egyptian upper-class families, such as the Boutros Boutros-Ghalis. Did you know that Boutros Boutros-Ghali was married to a Jew, Leah Nadler? I saw them in New York when he was Secretary-General at the United Nations.

Now I will tell you about the village of Gorizia. It was located on the Slovenian side of what today is the Slovenian-Italian border, and droves of domestic workers (some of them wet nurses) left from this village for Egypt. Because a large population settled in Alexandria from the mid-nineteenth century until some years after the Second World War, these maids were called "Aleksandrinke." They were protected by a Slavic association that provided them with free medical care as well as social assistance, should they need it. Evidently, those who came on their own were met by members of this association at the port of Alexandria and found community among them. My father told us how they traveled back and forth, and how some returned to marry while others stayed and grew old in Egypt. All this travel was done by ship.

Father had a passion for sea travel. He read extensively on the subject and larded our mealtime conversations with stories and trivia about who came to Alexandria, from where, and what ships they traveled on. He recounted how he and Mother sailed to Trieste and then traveled to Vienna to liquidate their assets in 1921, returning on the same ship that carried the Egyptian delegation sent to Paris to sign the peace treaty after World War I.

"Did you know that the Austrian Lloyd's first ship sailed to Istanbul on her maiden voyage in 1837?" Father would ask. "Did you know that steamers depart Trieste every Thursday at eleven thirty a.m., arriving in Alexandria the following Monday morning at six o'clock?" He informed us that *The Egyptian Gazette* printed its economic supplement to dovetail with the Austrian Lloyd scheduled departures to Europe to ensure timely distribution of the paper. That's how reliable they were, Father said, adding, "Their ships run like clockwork!" He chuckled as his choice of words was deliberate, clockwork alluding to his business: making and selling clocks and timepieces.

I must tell you, I do not have a clear idea of why my family chose to move to Egypt, but am trying to piece it together, just like my mother taught me to piece together bits of fabric to make decorative pillow slips and table runners while also teaching me how to sew dresses for myself. She would say, "You tell me you want a new dress, Adina? I'll help you make one, but you must persevere. Let's go shopping for fabric and start. If you spoil the fabric, it's all right; it's part of learning. We'll get more and start over. The key to success is to not give up." That is how Mother taught me to sew, and persevere.

There was a magazine shipped in from Germany to Alexandria at the time called *Deutsche Mode Zeitung*, which printed catalogues and patterns.

Mother taught me how to trace and pin such patterns on fabric, saying, "Don't be afraid to cut, Adina. If you make a mistake, try again, and salvage what you can to make your original patchwork pillows." All this was said in Italian, which was the language we spoke at home. So, by trial and error—a lot of error!—I learned to cut and sew. To this day I enjoy creating patchwork pieces, which I give as gifts. Mother loved sewing, as I'm sure you've guessed by now, but never on Friday because Fridays we prepared for the Sabbath. Cooking was done ahead of time and coffee—really chicory, not coffee beans—was prepared to fill our blue thermos bottle in readiness for the next day. That thermos has a story, which I'll tell you later.

In any case, when my parents decided to move to Egypt, there were evidently many business and investment opportunities. This, I understood, was thanks to Mohammad Ali, who became governor in the 1800s and jump-started Egypt into the modern age. Immigrants from Europe and the Mediterranean flocked to Egypt, attracted by the possibilities, the promise of tax exemptions and legal privileges for foreigners. Perhaps this is why my family came too, seeking opportunities, seeking their fortune. I suspect they may have had more intimate reasons as well for distancing themselves from the European continent. They never said so outright, but I have wondered if Albert and Lalita decided to steer clear of the Landolfis, who apparently never gave up aiming their barbs at Father, calling him "the Viennese clockmaker." Be that as it may, their decision offered the young couple a life of privilege, which they shared with my grandmother and Uncle Edgar. Of course, living in Egypt at this time, people were spared the horrors suffered by the Jews of Europe. There were troubled times in Egypt too, of course. We were pushed out in the 1940s and 1950s, but that is a story for later. I will tell you the story of Father and Uncle Edgar's arrest and incarceration during World War I, which had nothing to do with their being Jews.

During the years of World War I, Father and Uncle Edgar were arrested and sent to camps. They were detained by the British because they refused to give up their Austrian citizenship, which made them the enemy of the British, who at that time ruled Egypt. When war was declared they were given the option of purchasing a Turkish passport for fifteen Egyptian pounds, but would not do it. They insisted that they were Austrians and proud of it. Well, their pride landed them in a British internment camp at Sidi Bishr from 1914 to 1919.

Here is what I can tell you about the camps. The detainees were housed in military-style tents, Uncle Edgar and Father in one together. Sidi Bishr was far from town at that time, in the desert, along the Mediterranean. Today, Alexandria's population has ballooned and Sidi Bishr is as built-up as the rest of the city. Then, you had to travel what seemed like a long distance to get to this out-of-the-way place. My mother called Sidi Bishr "the place God has forgotten." In reality, it is a beautiful coastal neighborhood.

During the years Father was detained, Mother frequently took a train to Sidi Bishr Station. I was not yet born, but she repeated the story of her conjugal visits so often that I feel as if I was there along with my two sisters. Mother said that holding the hands of my sisters Alina and Alicia, one on either side of her, they walked to the camp and stood outside so Father could see them. "Sometimes we hired donkeys and rode to the camp," Mother added. Mother, who was an excellent seamstress, had designed and tailored a red suit for herself and matching red dresses and hats for each of my sisters. She said, "I chose red so that Father could see us coming from a long way off."

Once a month, conjugal visits were allowed and Sidi Bishr took on an almost festive air. The men bathed and shaved and tidied up their tents, and the women arrived with hampers of food and personal items for husbands, fathers, brothers. Alicia and Alina did not go at such times. They stayed home with Oma. Instead, Mother took the train, accompanied by Aunt Daria, Uncle Edgar's wife. They set out at dawn to have as much time with their husbands as possible. Years later, Aunt Daria remembered the contraband wine she and Mother spirited into camp. She and my mother would giggle like girls as they reminisced: "Remember the guards, Lalita? Remember how we gave them food and money? They were so grateful; good boys, really. But the wine, oh the wine, and those innocent-looking thermos bottles!" So this is where the story of the blue thermos comes in. I still have that old blue thermos bottle with the glass insert, which was filled with coffee for the Sabbath but used to sneak in wine on visiting days at Sidi Bishr. We were not allowed to take much when we left Egypt, but I managed to pack the thermos in my suitcase, wrapped in a sweater, and Daria did the same with hers, which was silver. I also took a few of my first books from Cité du Livre, small mementos of family history and my childhood.

Speaking of thermos bottles, I am reminded of another bit of trivia Father dished up: "Did you know, girls, that the thermos bottle was first called a vacuum flask and was invented in England in 1892?"

"Yes, Father!" we shouted. "And *thermos* comes from the Greek word *therme*, meaning hot!

Father smiled then. Yes, we were his girls.

At home, without Father, business began to falter and Mother resorted to selling stock from the shop as well as precious items from our home in order to support us. When Father was released from camp in 1919, the shop had collapsed. Despite these hardships, Mother was able to retain Elvira, who remained loyal to our family until her death. "Sometimes, she worked for no pay," Mother said, "but we made it up to her in later years."

My father, who was a craftsman, made all sorts of things while at the internment camp. He was there for years and had to keep his hands busy, he said. One item, which I still have, was a box made from cigar boxes, inlaid with Mother's initials with silver and copper by some method Father figured out using coins. He apparently gave it to her on one of their conjugal visits, but Edgar bested him. Aunt Daria gave birth to cousin Enrique nine months after this visit. Edgar and Daria decided to name the baby after the great opera singer, Enrico Caruso. They both loved opera, and Enrique actually became an opera singer. I went to hear him sing at the Metropolitan Opera in New York, years later.

Have I told you yet how Mother and Father fell in love and married? Let me tell you now.

Father met Mother at a *thé dansant* (tea dance) in Vienna. She had traveled from Trieste with one of her sisters to visit a cousin and was there for an entire season, several months. At that time, people did not just stay a week or a few days, you see, and quite possibly Lalita's family had some prospective bridegrooms in mind for her. Instead, she met Father and it was love at first sight. Apparently, Father dared not ask her to dance, as they had not been formally introduced. He did follow her home, however, to find out who she was and where she lived, and appealed to a friend who knew the family to make introductions before she returned to Trieste. I can only imagine that they must have courted at her cousin's before he traveled to Trieste to see her again and to meet her parents. One thing is sure: Father did not waste time in asking for Lalita's hand in marriage. Although Father's family was prosperous, Mother's felt they were a cut above. Mother came from a family of bankers who had high hopes for their daughter and wanted her to marry within their circle. She finally wore down their resistance and they grudgingly agreed to her marriage to Albert. Soon after, they left for Egypt.

When my parents and grandmother boarded the ship bound for Alexandria, little did they know what destiny held in store for them. They had not liquidated all of their assets in Europe and I wondered if they were perhaps intending to return to Vienna.

Before I was born, they had established themselves in Alexandria, where, as it turned out, they spent the rest of their lives. Their journey from Europe had been uneventful. Soon after they arrived, Father established his business and Oma her medical practice. Here is how it happened.

A client of Father's in Vienna, a wealthy Egyptian aristocrat, had found them a house close to Sharia Fuad, as Mother had said she liked to live close to downtown. This was where they began their married life in Egypt and where I was born. From our rooftop you could see the Mediterranean in the distance, a view we all loved.

When I was old enough to understand, Oma told my sisters and me that she felt she had considerably more freedom and ease of movement as an educated, professional woman in Alexandria than she did in Vienna. She was treated with deference and respect, gaining the veneration of her patients and their families. She loved her life in Egypt and liked to point out that Egyptian women had more rights than their European counterparts: "Women by law can hold on to their properties here; even fellaheen (peasant) women who have property, like Fatima, the *bawwab's* (doorman's) wife, who receives a yearly income from the fig trees she owns near Marsa Matruh, even though her land is tended by her brothers. It's hers to do with as she wishes." Grandmother had learned to speak Arabic and gathered many interesting stories as she took care of her patients. As she dedicated a portion of her practice to poor women, she was cherished by the families whose babies she delivered, receiving no pay. In fact, a story circulated that she tucked coins under the pillows of nursing mothers so their families could buy chickens to make soup for them. "Chicken soup fortifies," Oma would declare, and was pleased when fathers, brothers, and husbands thanked her by saying, "You're the equal of a hundred men!"

Among the people my grandmother met through her medical practice was a wealthy Coptic landowner who made a tradition of sending us a live lamb yearly by way of expressing his gratitude for the medical care Oma gave his family. One year he sent two. It was at the time of World War II, summer of 1942, I think, and Alexandria was apparently at risk. Mother pleaded with Father to take us to a bomb shelter. He sent us, but he refused to go himself, instructing Sayyid, our most trusted servant, instead to accompany us to the neighborhood shelter. "If I die, I'll die in my own bed. You take the children and go," he said to Mother. But since he would not go, she stayed too, sending us with the trusted Sayyid, who was in charge, along with our nanny. We had started down the street when Mother called Sayyid back, saying, "Take the lambs, too." I shall never forget the scene as long as I live. Here I was with my sisters, Elvira, Sayyid, Fatima, their three children, and the two bleating lambs, proceeding down the sidewalk in single file to take shelter from bombs, which in the end never reached us. I think that people's fears were to some extent alleviated by our droll band. In the end, we all returned home safely, the Germans were defeated by the British at the gates of Alexandria, and on the radio we heard Churchill say that this was not the end, but the end of the beginning. I don't really know why I remember this detail because, while it left an impression on my young mind, I did not really understand what he meant.

Women of Oma's class rarely worked then, but Oma Grete had no patience for keeping house, playing cards, shopping, going to the seam-stress or the tailor and the hat maker, leading a life of leisure as did so many of the women of her class and so many in Mother's circle of acquaintances. She instilled this appreciation of a life of purpose in her granddaughters, saying, "You can marry and have children, but remember that you can also have a profession that will serve you, give you a backbone, provide you with satisfaction. Exercise your wits, girls, and put your gifts to good use, and you will experience the thrill of being free and able." She always concluded these little talks with: "Remember my words after I'm gone." And we did.

Shortly after their arrival in Egypt, two daughters were born: my sisters Alina and Alicia. Mother miscarried with her third and fourth pregnancies, and then, lo and behold, I made my appearance. I was not expected. As my sisters grew up, married, and left home, my father would say to Mother, "Wouldn't we have had a sad nest if all of our girls had learned to fly at the same time, my dear Lita?" This was his affectionate nickname for her. She would respond, "Thank goodness we still have Adina!"

We were a close-knit, happy family but, of course, it was normal for my sisters to leave and start families of their own and to not be with us daily. However, we were in each other's houses often and met for meals at least once a week and always for the holidays.

The holiday I loved best was Hanukkah, because it was a festival of light and because it sometimes coincided with my birthday. My earliest memory of Hanukkah was of watching my mother light the candles with the helper candle, the shammash. I loved our menorah softly glowing in the living room window, and the prayers.

The Hanukkah prayer I first learned was, "*Baruch atah Adonai Elohenu, melekh ha'olam, shehecheyanu vekiymanu vehigi'anu lazman hazeh.*" (Blessed are You, Lord, our God, King of the Universe, who has granted us life, sustained us, and enabled us to reach this occasion.) We said this prayer on the first night.

I loved all of the holidays and the seasons, but it was Hanukkah that had a special place in my heart as a child, an adult, a married woman. It remains my favorite.

I married a Sephardic Jew, Albaz Hadar, named after his paternal grandfather. My parents had reservations about him since they would have preferred an Ashkenazi Jew for a son-in-law. In time, they grew to appreciate and cherish Albaz, however. He had a gentle nature, fortitude, and dedication to his faith, and was devoted to family. He was a scholar and also a go-getter, and won over my entire family.

Albaz studied law and became a successful attorney. He held as his role model the Sephardic chief rabbi of Egypt, Haim Nahum Effendi. Rabbi Nahum was born in Turkey in 1872, and this is why he received the title effendi, a Turkish title given him to indicate esteem and to honor him. Rabbi Nahum himself was a scholar and lawyer, a linguist and diplomat. He was the erudite advocate for a community of eighty thousand Jews living in Egypt when he was chief rabbi. He served as religious leader to the community from 1925 until his death. With heartbreak, he witnessed his community dwindle, along with his health and eyesight. Rabbi Nahum died in 1960 but was never forgotten, continuing to be recognized and cherished by Middle Eastern Jews the world over.

The year of Rabbi Nahum's death, Albaz and I began to think in earnest of quitting Egypt, and ultimately cast our lot with that of our siblings and other family members migrating to the United States, making New York—well,

Brooklyn to be exact—our new home. As we had no children of our own, Albaz and I nurtured close bonds with our nieces and nephews, and have remained close to our families both geographically and emotionally. Albaz studied for and passed the New York bar exam and established a law practice in Brooklyn. Meanwhile, I taught French and enrolled as a student and a PhD candidate at City University of New York. My doctorate is in comparative literature. I enjoyed teaching for years and am now enjoying my retirement and the piles of books I have gathered to read, my new companions.

Had it not been for the mounting pressures on Jews in the 1940s, the repercussions on our communities after the creation of the state of Israel, the Egyptian Revolution of 1952, the confiscation and sequestration of Jewish assets and properties, the persecutions, we might never have left. You see, for us, life in Egypt was sweet. It was not only the land of our births but the setting where we spent happy childhoods, married, raised families. Our parents and grandparents, all of those we cherished, are buried in Egyptian soil. We lived and prospered in Egypt, and Egypt embraced us until we began to feel the pinch of anti-Semitism and eventually had to leave. Some left of their own free will, others were expelled.

I was not quite twenty, I think, when I became aware that all was not well for the Jews of Egypt. In 1945, we heard about attacks on the Jewish quarter in Cairo and the burning of a synagogue. In 1947, something called the Companies Law was put into effect, limiting to very few the number of non-Egyptian employees a business could hire, including Jews. Most of us never bothered to take Egyptian citizenship and some who would have done so when discrimination against non-Egyptians grew no longer could. My sister Aline lost her job as an accountant in a textile mill where she had worked for a decade as the noose tightened around our necks. Though we Jews were an integral and respected part of Egypt's social fabric, we began to feel threatened. It did not matter that we had been in Egypt for generations, like the Qattawi family, with whom we were acquainted. They claimed to have lived in Egypt since the eighth century! There were others of the same ilk. Of course, Moses was an Egyptian. Still, any way you looked at it, it was increasingly evident that a Jewish presence in Egypt was an alien presence. We gradually became the enemy, no longer regarded as threads in the fabric of Egyptian society.

Father had sold his business prior to the great troubles, and a timely decision it was. His assets would surely have been frozen or seized. He managed our resources in such a way as to make it possible for us to continue to live decently on the income he generated from the sale. We found ways to cope and Father reminded us of the great king Solomon's wisdom: The righteous one falls seven times and rises again. And so we did.

In 1948 emergency law was declared, which forbade Egyptians and also Jews from leaving the country without a special permit called an exit visa. For us, it was a double-edged sword. On the one hand we were aliens and on the other hand we had to submit to the same restrictions as Egyptian citizens and could not leave without official permission. During this period, hundreds of Jews were arrested and their properties confiscated, and though my family stayed under the radar, we were deeply worried, of course. However, we experienced a brief resurgence of hope in 1950 when Jewish detainees were released and properties restored. This decision had strings attached: Jews must donate money to military efforts and denounce the state of Israel. Those who did not comply met with consequences. They were arrested along with communists and others considered subversive, enemies of the state.

In 1952, after the revolution and the ousting of King Faruq, General Muhammad Naguib headed a new government. A sense of hope reemerged as this benign leader showed himself to be favorably inclined toward the Jews. This respite was short-lived as, in the winter of 1954, Gamal Abd al-Nasser seized power and our situation grew dire. We considered leaving then, but Oma Grete was too frail to travel and Mother was in poor health. Instead, we held fast to hope, to our faith, and to each other. When Mother died right after Rosh Hashanah, which fell in September that year of 1958, we knew Father would not survive her loss, and he indeed died in December, right after Yom Kippur. Oma had died two years before at the age of seventy-four, after a productive life as a healer and after dedicating herself to safely delivering so many Alexandrian babies. People who remembered her spoke of her affectionately, despite the chill that was descending from all sides upon the backs of Jews. Few were willing to stand up for us, their words growing ever fainter, and those who remembered the good times were either dead or buried in sandstorms of hostility. We had stayed longer than most in our community and we knew the time had come to act, to go.

Our cousin Alma lived in New York. When we heard the bell toll for us, we reached out to her for help. She was by then an American citizen and could sponsor us. Alma had married Mordecai, a New Yorker who visited

Egypt in 1939 in search of business opportunities, staying one year. They met, married in 1940, and returned to raise a family of six children in the United States. They lived in Brooklyn Heights and prospered. Through the years, we stayed in touch, especially around holidays and family events like births and deaths. We wrote letters back and forth, exchanging news. When it looked like we could be in danger, Alma sent the following telegram, which I still have:

"Come at once STOP No room for hesitation STOP Open arms await STOP Love A."

I have it framed on my desk to remind me of Alma's sentiments and the tears that greeted her generous offer to shelter us and help us start a new life. Alma made the path clear for us.

In December of 1960, my sisters called a family council. We passed Alma's telegram around and discussed our options. Albaz and I, his mother and siblings, Uncle Edgar, Aunt Daria, Enrique (their only son), Alicia and her family, all agreed to meet for lunch at Alina's to decide on what to do. We agreed then and there to take a leap of faith, to ready ourselves to confront our destinies, to leave Egypt for a new world, just as our parents and grandmother had done years earlier when they left Europe.

When I asked Albaz, "What choice do we have?" he said, "We have strength in numbers and the support of a tight-knit family. We can start over anywhere."

We ourselves were not harmed in Egypt, but all around us we saw arrests of other Jews, most of them detained for their political ideals and activities. Some reported being tortured.

On the streets, in front of Jewish shops and synagogues, we witnessed shouts, slurs, threats. We knew we had to leave. When we applied for exit visas, a necessary permit allowing anyone to leave the country, they were delivered expeditiously. The following words were stamped on each exit visa: "*Bidun rugu'*," meaning without the option of returning.

Our emotions ran high. We wept knowing our exit was final. We were abandoning all that was familiar to us. We were leaving behind our dead at the Mazarita cemetery. Who would tend to their graves? Our hearts were heavy.

Albaz took it upon himself to be the 'consoler' of the family. He reminded us that Jewish law seeks to encourage mourners not to dwell too long on death, rather to concentrate on bonding with life. But our hearts were heavy. How would we endure the finality of this departure?

We gathered together as a family, prior to leaving. We made our last visit to the cemetery in the month of August. It was Tisha Bav, a day of fasting, commemorating disasters faced by the Jewish people throughout history. We placed stones on the graves, prayed, said goodbye to our dead, and before we knew it, Egypt was behind us.

This was our final prayer, said with gravity and emotion at the Mazarita cemetery:

"Baruch atah Adonai Elohenu, melekh ha'olam asher yatzar etchem badin, v'dan v'chilkail etchem badin, v'hemit etchem badin, v'yodeah mispar koolchem badin, v'atid l'hachazir ulhachayot etchem badin. Baruch atah adonaim'chayeh hemetim." (Praised be the Eternal, our God, the Ruler of the Universe who created you in judgment, who maintained and sustained you in judgment, who brought death upon you in judgment, who knows the deeds of each one of you in judgment, and who will hereafter restore you to life in judgment. Praised be the Eternal who will restore life to the dead.)

We ushered in 1961 on American soil. We were armed with courage and ready to face the future. There was a period of adjustment, of course. We did very well and found ourselves settling easily in the new world. When Albaz died, he left a huge hole in my heart, but left me well provided for. I have focused on the happiness we experienced rather than on the losses.

I must retrace my steps, though, and tell you a bit more about our lives prior to New York.

My father, Albert Adler, was born in Vienna at a time when Austria had a significant Jewish population, more than one-hundred thousand in Vienna alone, I believe. The Jews had a long history in this region of the world and Vienna was a center of Jewish culture, until the advent of the religiously and politically motivated anti-Semitism of the 1930s, and the invasion of Austria by the German armies in March 1938, which sounded the Jewish community's death knell. My father and mother were long gone by then, and were probably not fully aware of the scale of the violence directed at Jews and of the horrors taking place in Europe.

My father's family were jewelers who specialized in clocks and timepieces. He was very skilled with his hands and carried with him to Egypt the business traditions of his family. In Alexandria, he started his own business.

He made jewelry, imported clocks and fine watches, and trained Edgar, who was a decade younger, to work with him.

After World War I, Father quit the jewelry business. He and Edgar became partners and began importing bentwood furniture as well as toys. I enjoyed a lot of dolls, dollhouses and doll furniture as a result. After a while, Mother didn't know what to do with all of my toys and sent me up to the attic to play. It was not exactly an attic as you find in homes here in the United States, but something we called a *sandara*, a sort of low-ceilinged storage room, a loft, reached by climbing a drop-down ladder. Keep in mind that ceilings in old Egyptian houses were very high, some as high as twelve feet.

I have one particularly vivid memory of playing up in that little attic. One day my eldest sister decided to come up and see what I was doing. Like Mother, she was tall, but was more solidly built. She climbed up, squeezed in behind me, and then couldn't turn around to come down. She twisted uncomfortably to get her legs in position to reach for the ladder. When she touched the rungs and looked down, she panicked. She was in fact afraid of heights and began to scream. It was a comical scene that we did not let her forget. As my sister screamed, I yelled for help. We both melted into uncontrollable laughter and tears until Father came to the rescue. He tugged and pulled her, finally supporting her down the ladder until she reached the ground. When I remember that day, I think of the Winnie-the-Pooh stories I read as a child. Do you remember how Pooh got stuck in the window of his house after getting too fat eating too much honey? Pooh and Babar were favorite book characters of my childhood. I also enjoyed *La Semaine de Suzette*, a magazine my sisters collected, featuring an amusing little Breton maid called Bécassine.

Because I was younger than my sisters, they babied me. I particularly loved it when they read to me. Sometimes one or the other would let me crawl into bed with her for bedtime stories. Our beds were arranged along three walls of a spacious bedroom, with a dresser and an armoire on the fourth wall. I had crawled into bed with one of my sisters one night when I was startled awake by a bad dream. She comforted me and I fell asleep. I must have squirmed and kicked her, so she left me in her bed and crawled into mine. The beds were against walls on opposite sides of the room, and in the middle of the night, I started to cry. My sister woke up and tried to get out of bed, but kept running into a wall, having forgotten which side of the room she was on. We all woke, but were groggy and panicked. We started screaming. Mother, Father, and Nanny came running, switched on the lights, and found us trying to push away the walls in an effort to get out of bed. What bedlam!

At home my mother spoke Italian. In fact, we all spoke Italian. It was the language we used daily, even though my father's first language was German and he spoke French fluently as well as Italian. Well, we all spoke French. Father went a step further and took courses in Arabic, which he learned to speak, read, and write—classical Arabic. He loved learning and had a facility with languages that Mother did not possess. She spoke no Arabic to speak of save a smattering of what we called "shopkeeper Arabic."

When I married Albaz, I applied myself to learning the language of his family. Arabic was what my sweet mother-in-law spoke. She took me into the kitchen "to learn the language of cooking," she said, and patiently corrected my mistakes. Eventually, I became quite proficient in the Arabic of the homemaker, although I never learned to read or write it.

There were many Austrian visitors to Alexandria long before I was born, and while I was growing up. Father told of the visit of Emperor Franz Joseph, also of Archduke Ludwig Salvator.

He wintered in Alexandria in the 1900s and wrote a book, which Father had. It was titled *Ramleh als Winteraufenthal* (Ramleh as a Winter Resort), in which he described the climate, flora, fauna, houses, and streets of Ramleh, stretching from Sidi Gaber to Montazah, and east of Alexandria all the way to Abukir. It is perhaps strange that we never listened to jazz or anything but classical music, and certainly never Arabic music. We were steeped in European culture and had very little to do with our geographical environment, its culture, or its people, except perhaps in visiting sites of pharaonic history. We existed, lived, and thrived in modern Egypt, this land and people who welcomed us then tossed us out. How sad that we lived apart as we did. Well, not quite apart. We led, you might say, parallel lives, and enjoyed the opportunities Egypt offered us. Barring a few upper-class Egyptian families, our friends were mostly Europeans. This mindset was the mindset of most Europeans living in Egypt at that time. We loved Egypt, but rarely mixed with Egyptians. When I had been in the United States long enough for the bitter taste of our imposed departure to fade, I realized just how much I missed Egypt and our lives there. As an established New Yorker, I began to search for the sights and smells and feel of my childhood. I strolled through the Egyptian galleries at the

Metropolitan Museum, and drove weekly to Sahadi's Middle Eastern food store on Atlantic Avenue to get a whiff of the spices and the foods offered in this quintessential Brooklyn establishment. The smells, the energy, the banter I encountered warmed my heart and senses, and of course I came away loaded with foods that took me back to my childhood. Today, so much of what I experience opens the floodgates of memory. In some ways, I am more drawn to Egypt today than I ever was when I lived there and my gaze was turned toward Europe. Now I seem to have come full circle.

3
Ester

Meeting Ester

I met Ester at the Ninety-Second Street YMCA in New York City. I had gone with a friend to hear Elie Wiesel speak on the Book of Ruth in the Bible. My friend knew Ester and beckoned to her to join us when she saw her enter the lecture hall. After the lecture, we all three went to get coffee nearby and I told Ester that I had begun to collect stories of Egyptian Jews. She was interested and invited me to tea, saying, "I'll make *karkade* for us. Do you remember this hibiscus tea we used to drink in Egypt? My father always ordered it from Aswan. We drank it all summer long and Mother claimed it lowered her blood pressure. I still love it. Do you?" I accepted her invitation and soon came back to record her story. Ester lived in a small apartment not far from the Ninety-Second Street Y. I took the bus up from the East Village, where I was living at the time, tape recorder, extra batteries, and tapes in the black backpack I carried all over the city. Arriving, I pushed open the exterior door and pressed the button on the building's intercom. Ester answered "*Meeeean?*" (Who is it?) We both laughed at this Egyptianism and she buzzed me in. She stood at the door, the foyer of her apartment was dark and smelling a little of mothballs. She welcomed me in Arabic, saying, "*ahlan wa sahlan*" (welcome), and I smiled and responded, "*ahlan beekee*" (may you be welcome). She loved hearing Arabic because it reminded her of her childhood in Cairo, she told me. Throughout the visit, she trotted out different sayings and proverbs, and I taught her a few more. We laughed a lot and, as with Vida and Adina, Egypt had clearly left its mark.

Ester was small and olive-skinned. She had fine features and must at one time have been doll-like pretty. She was roundish, barely five-foot tall, and jolly. Her brown eyes, flecked with gold, twinkled when she spoke, especially when she came out with an Arabic phrase she was pleased to have remembered. She was dressed in a lilac three-quarter-sleeve polyester blouse and a loose-fitting jumper of a color I could only think of as 'eggplant.' It looked homemade. She searched the patch pockets, each trimmed with a small bow, as if looking for something. Her hands came up empty, but the thin gold bracelets on her wrists jingled with every movement. She wore six on each arm, bringing to mind how village women in Egypt wore their wealth on their arms for safekeeping. Ester's bracelets tinkled and her eyes twinkled as she served us tea, which was indeed hibiscus, but made from a tea bag. A thin gold band on her left finger was the only other jewelry she wore.

I offered her a bouquet of carnations upon arrival. She sniffed them and placed them in what looked to be a hand-blown glass vase. It was not until some years later that she confessed to her aversion to carnations, saying, "They remind me of funerals, Nayra." When I visited her subsequently, I brought tulips, daisies, or some other seasonal blooms. But, on this first visit, I asked about her vase and she eagerly responded, no doubt avoiding embarrassing me about my choice of flowers. She said, "This glass is made in Mexico, but it reminds me so much of Egyptian Muski glass. Do you remember it?" I responded that I had a collection of little animals made of the same glass, which my mother had given me years ago. Ester jumped up and brought her own collection to show me. Clearly, we had grown up in the same town, going to some of the same places, shopping in the historic Muski district of Cairo with its spice, gold, glass, and brass markets, its narrow streets and narrow lanes forever etched in our memories. We chatted and compared notes, after which I asked permission to turn on my tape recorder. Ester put away the tea things and, almost in a whisper, she began to tell her story.

Ester tells her story

I was born in Cairo and was given the name of my paternal grandmother, Esther, but my name was spelled E-S-T-E-R. As an afterthought, an *a* was added at the end, making it sound like a diminutive of Esther. My name then became Estera, meaning little Esther, although everyone called me Ester, except when teasing or taunting me, when they stretched it to "Ees-Tay-Raaa, Ees-Tay-Raaaa, Ees-Tay-Raaaaa," and so on.

Over the years, I wondered if adding an *a* at the end of Ester was my mother's way of making it sound a bit like Sara, her mother's name, imbuing Ester with flavors of Sara. My mother, Salma, adored her mother, and family lore had it that Mother wanted to name me Sara, but Father insisted that his first daughter be given his mother's name. Could it be that Ester and Sara were made into Estera, a compromise? Who knows! People are always asking, "What's in a name?" Well, I say a lot. A name reveals who you are, defines you, is powerful. I believe it carries your destiny. Remember the story of the goddess Isis robbing the sun god Ra of his power as king of the gods by tricking him into revealing his name? Ra was an old man and had spittle leaking from his mouth. Isis took some, mixed it with clay, and created a serpent, which bit Ra and made him sick with its poison. Isis promised to heal him if he revealed his name to her. When he did, he also gave her power over him and she got him to abdicate in favor of Horus, her son, who then became king. So, in a sense, in giving over his name, he also gave up his destiny.

Over time, Mother told people that my name suited me because I was growing into a beautiful young woman just like the Hebrew queen Esther, who saved the Jews from extermination in ancient Persia. I memorized this verse recorded in the Book of Esther: "Now in the twelfth month, which is the month Adar, on the thirteenth day of the same, when the king's commandment and his decree drew near to be put in execution, in the day that the enemies of the Jews hoped to have rule over them; whereas it was turned to the contrary, that the Jews had rule over them that hated them . . . " Purim is the feast celebrating the Jewish people's deliverance from the harm the Persian king meant to inflict on them thanks to Esther's intercession. I loved celebrating Purim with my family because we got to dress up in costumes and exchange gifts, and I was given an extra gift on account of my name. Mother made a delicious meal and Father, who had learned some Hebrew at temple, always said this prayer after the meal: "*B'rich rahamana malka d'alma mareih d'hahy pita*," which means "Blessed are you merciful and omnipotent one, creator of this bread." Over time, perhaps at Mother's insistence, he said it after every meal.

Mother sometimes called me by the pet name Sarsura, giving Estera an affectionate twist while invoking Sara, whom we children fondly called Nena (Grandmother) Sarsura. I felt as if my mother were slathering on my heart not only my grandmother's name but her persona, willing me to grow up to be just like Sara, who was a tall, green-eyed beauty in a family of brown-eyed, olive-skinned people, some stocky like Nena Esther. I remained small, however, and my eyes, while flecked with a little green and gold, were brown. Mother resembled her father, Sidi (Grandfather) Aslan, who was dark and a little stout. She could not be called a beauty like Tante (Aunt) Yvette, her sister, who took after Nena Sara. But Mother had beautiful, smooth skin and beautiful hands; everyone said so.

When Mother called me her Sarsura, no one but Grandmother Esther took exception. If Father raised an eyebrow, Mother just laughed and hummed this made-up nonsense verse: "Sarsura, Sarsura, Sarsuuraaaaaa, she's going to ride a Hantuuraaaa (horse-drawn carriage)." My father had a sense of humor too, and chanted right back: "Sursaara (cockroach), Sursaara, Sursaaraaaaa, my little cockroach is not Sara," and so on. This had us all in stitches, but did not please Grandmother Esther, who was for a time living with us.

I saw the light of day at home, in the early hours of a summer morning in the neighborhood of Daher. It was largely populated at the time by Christians and Jews, though we had a few Muslim neighbors. Our apartment was in a part of Daher called Sakakini, named in recognition of Habib Sakakini Pasha (1841–1923), a prominent Egyptian who, as a teenager, had come from Syria to Egypt to seek his fortune. Some people said that his ancestors traded in swords and knives, and hence the family name Sakakini—knife or sword maker. He did indeed make his fortune, but not in knives or swords, rather in construction. It was said that he helped in the digging of the Suez Canal in some way, but I don't know if this is truth or rumor. When he got rich, he built a grand home, a rococo palace at the center of Midan Ibn Khaldun. It is the highest spot in Daher, eight streets radiating from it. He named his son and heir Henri, and named one of the streets Rue Henri. Henri, in turn, named his own daughter Henriette, not surprisingly, since middle-class Egyptians at the time were enamored by everything French, from names to Louis XVIth–style furniture. We, like many middle- and upper-class children, were brought up speaking French and Arabic, using them interchangeably or together. This word salad was typically Egyptian.

My family rented a fourth-floor apartment in a four-story building in Daher. These apartments were two to a floor, and had high ceilings and large rooms—three bedrooms, a tiny maid's room, and a living room with a glassed-off balcony to one side, which was enjoyed in winter, and where

Mother and Tante Yvette made all of us girls sit every Thursday afternoon to do some knitting, embroidering, or crochet work. I remember that she bought needles and DMC thread in bulk, imported from France. Each girl had her own thimble and sewing kit, and was expected to finish a defined piece of work before being released to go out with friends, as on Thursdays we had only a half-day of school. I hated these sessions and had a hard time sitting still. I'd drum up any excuse to go on an errand, saying to Mother, "I'm going to step out to buy some more thread, or thread of a different color, or my needle broke, I'm missing this or that . . . " Mother responded, "Already? You've barely sat down!" But, she said it in Arabic: "*Inti ma-l-hi'teesh!*" I must admit that eventually the discipline of these Thursday afternoons stood me in good stead when we had to leave Egypt and I needed to find work to tide us over. We left later than most, in 1961.

Like most middle-class Cairo apartments of the day, ours had one bathroom, with a tub, sink, bidet, and a toilet in a separate cubicle. The servants used a Turkish-style toilet in a room on the roof, which also had a spigot and a big zinc tub for their use. On the other side of the apartment was a fair-sized kitchen and balcony. Mother and Tante Yvette lived in the same building, on the same floor. Our kitchens were across a narrow landing from each other, accessed by a set of narrow metal steps coming up from the back of the building. That's where the *zabbalin* (garbage collectors, often children, really) came to take away our detritus, which was placed outside the kitchen door. They carried an *ooffa* (soft, two-handled hamper woven from palm fronds). They came once a week, accepting what payment each tenant chose to make for their service. We found out subsequently that they were Christians, kept pigs, and recycled much of what they collected, feeding pigs with kitchen leavings. If the *bawwab* (door-keeper) of the building came up to the apartments, he too used those back steps, calling out, "*Ya sitt, ya sitt*," (miss, miss) or "*Ya Adiba*" (the maid) while standing outside the kitchen door.

It was wonderful for us cousins to live so tribally: family and playmates all rolled into one. The doors of both kitchens were often left open all day, allowing us to go back and forth freely. We played, fought, made up, scrapped, and cavorted at will. Our households were in constant motion and commotion, and we children pretty much did as we pleased, except on Thursday afternoons when the girls were instructed in sewing, embroidery, knitting, crochet, and on Friday nights when Mother lit the candles and we celebrated Shabbat. These were sacred. Of course, on feast days the families got together for elaborately prepared meals.

I remember sneaking out one Thursday, however. I had seen an announcement that Gary Cooper was coming to town and staying at the Shepheard's Hotel. I found some excuse to miss the handwork afternoon with Mother, Tante Yvette, and the girls, and went out with my friend Marianna to see him. When we got to Shepheard's we asked for his room number, went up, and knocked on the door, but no one answered. We turned the knob and the door opened. On a table was a huge bouquet of flowers. We tiptoed in, plucked two roses from the bouquet, and rushed out, giggling all the way home. The next day, we made our schoolmates jealous when we boasted that Gary Cooper had given us each a rose. Another time, a group of us attended a performance by the Comedie Française at the Khedivial Royal Opera House, where Verdi's *Aida* had its debut on December 24, 1871, marking the opening of the Suez Canal. Unfortunately, the Opera burned to the ground in October 1971, just shy of a full hundred years after the performance of the opera written for its inauguration. The structure was made entirely of wood and was a jewel box of a theater. As a teen, I had a big crush on the French actor Charles Boyer, and when he came to Cairo I went to see him perform at the Opera. Then, going backstage, I asked him to autograph his photo. "Please add two words," I pleaded. He signed his photo with the following dedication: "To Ester, in friendship, offered with a couple of words." He wrote it in French, of course: "*Avec deux mots qui sont deux mots de sympathie, Charles Boyer.*" I still have this signed black-and-white portrait of him. When I look at it, it floods my heart with longing, taking me back to afternoons and evenings spent with friends, with not a worry in the world, and certainly no thought that the Egyptian world we grew up in, knew, and loved would one day be shattered, sending us wandering all over again, like the Jews of olden days.

Tante Yvette, who was one year younger than Mother, had married the same year as her. They were sixteen- and fifteen-year-old brides. Tante Yvette and Uncle Elam, her husband, had seven children, three girls and four boys, alternating boy, girl, boy, and finally two boys one after the other. We were three girls first, and finally a boy, whom my parents named Amran after the father of the prophet Moses who led the Jewish people out of Egypt. This is a bit of irony as my parents, and particularly my father, never wanted to leave Egypt, nor would have guessed at the time of Amran's birth that we ever would.

I'm proud to say that when my brother was born and my parents rejoiced at finally having a son, I was not jealous. Rather, I was protective of Amran, though I teased him a lot. Once, I asked him if he wanted me to tell him whom he would marry. He said yes. I said, "You'll have to give me one of your toys." So he did, and waited for me to reveal to him his future bride. I said, "*Adiba!*" (The maid). He was furious and threw a building block at my head and grazed the side of my cheek. It was not a grave injury, but I made sure to play it up to the hilt, crying and accusing him of being a murderer. He was stricken with guilt and the full weight of his crime. I gained power over him because of this and could get him to do whatever I wanted for months after the incident. As adults, we joked about it for years, laughing so hard tears sprang from our eyes.

We children called Tante Yvette by the moniker *La Tayyeba* (mixing Arabic and French, as was commonly done). It means the 'kind one' in Arabic, which was apt because she yielded to our whims, fed us sweets, and tolerated (maybe even enjoyed) our pranks. We had cats and, oddly enough, we never named them, just calling them all *otta* (cat). One game we played involved hiding the cats in a closet and watching as Tante Yvette discovered them. We called this game "search and liberate." Tante Yvette pretended to stumble on the cats when opening a closet door, jumping back in mock surprise, then shaking an accusing finger at us. We lured her into our games and mischief and she loved to laugh with us. She was a little childlike and was a prankster herself, sneaking an onion or an apple into her pocket at the greengrocer's or making off with a Poulain chocolate bar from the candy store around the corner. She giggled and showed Mother her loot and Mother made her return or pay for what she had purloined. She was docile and did as she was told. The neighborhood shopkeepers liked her and turned a blind eye to her antics, smiling knowingly, calling her *maskeena*, a poor thing, one whom God had made this way. Egyptians were a very tolerant people, and these shopkeepers knew Mother would make sure they got paid. I think her youth, fair complexion, and sparkling eyes made Tante Yvette look innocent, and really, she was.

Our pranks varied according to our whims. One holiday season, when there was much activity in both kitchens, we spirited away a roast from Tante Yvette's kitchen and put it in Mother's. When our aunt discovered the meat was missing, her face flushed pink as it always did if she was fussed. She searched high and low for that missing roast and finally called to Mother across the landing: "Salma, Salma, the cats stole the meat!" We promptly emerged from our hiding places to offer help, but Mother knew full well who the cats really were: Adiba, our Sudanese maid, had seen us and told. The meat was under a layer of my father's *Al-Ahram* newspaper, in Mother's *namliya*. This *namliya* was a feature of just about every kitchen at the time, a place to keep foods cool and away from insects, even rodents, although in our houses *otta* encouraged mice, rats, and even ferrets, plentiful in Cairo, to keep their distance. It was a very practical screened food pantry designed to allow for air circulation. Some families had zinc-lined iceboxes too, but they were small. The blocks of ice needed replenishing every few days and took up half the icebox, so the *namliya* was used for overflow. People shopped daily for food anyway. Mother planned her menus for a week and it was Father who always shopped for meat and fish. There was an ambulant fishmonger near his shop in Hamzawi. Sometimes he bought the "catch of the day" from this man. Other times, he went to al-Attaba al-Khadra, a huge market where a better variety of fish could be found. The part of the fish he and my sister Abigail relished was the head. It was steamed and served to them drizzled with oil and lemon juice, salt and pepper. Father picked out the cheeks and exclaimed, "*Ya salam, da mazaag!*" "What a treat!" The word *mazaag*, however, has a very particular meaning in Arabic, and indicates something we do, eat, or drink that satisfies a mood. Food was fresh and only dry goods were stored for any length of time. But, getting back to our prank, Mother dressed us down sharply after making us own up to our shenanigans. She said she was putting us on bread and water that night. We tried to act contrite, but it had been so much fun that we couldn't stop giggling. Besides, we knew Mother would not make good on her threats because Tante Yvette would intervene on our behalf. She always did.

I was the most rascally of all my cousins. My mother, at her wits end with me one summer, appealed to Father to do something about this *'afreeta*, this little devil. School was out, my brother was still nursing, Mother was exhausted, and there was no Tante Yvette to distract me as she always could. She and her family had gone ahead of us to set up our *'eshash* (huts) at Ras al-Barr, where we vacationed for a month every summer. For some reason, I had been left behind with Mother, who would follow a week later with Father, my baby brother, and Adiba. Our servant Amin had gone ahead to help my aunt prepare our camp.

I loved Ras al-Barr and the *'eshash* made of wood and reeds, erected in summer only for vacationers. I loved the donkeys we rode along the beach and the tenor of life with no pressures whatsoever. This spot was unique; the Nile met the Mediterranean there at Ras al-Barr, creating a most unusual scene. Sand and alluvium formed beaches of fine silty sand, dark in color and said to be rejuvenating. I think it was the relaxed life that benefited us most, but we took sand baths as recommended for health and healing anyway. At midday, we dug big holes in the sand and buried ourselves in them for an hour or so, then washed off in the salty, silty water and returned to the huts to eat and nap. But I digress . . .

The summer I'm telling you about, I was left behind in Cairo with Mother. She grew so tired of my shenanigans and moodiness that she asked Father to take me to work with him. In his store, bolts of cotton poplin shirting were stacked on shelves and carefully labeled and numbered according to color. I took it into my head to reorganize them, and removed the labels, thinking I would re-mark the bolts. This unwanted help caused Father and his employees great consternation when they apprehended me and made me stop. They had to re-label everything I had 'helped with' and lost precious time undoing my mischief. After this day, Father refused to take me to work with him ever again. Soon after, however, we were on our way to Ras al-Barr and all was forgotten.

On Sundays, when we were old enough to go out in groups of young people, Father sometimes drove me and a friend or friends to a theater called the Kursaal. Once, having failed to check what was playing and just wanting to be out of the house, we landed in the midst of a group of Greeks, who laughed uproariously throughout the show while we understood nothing. The performance was a Greek comedy. We tried asking the couple sitting next to us for translation, but they glared at us and said in French, "Why come to a Greek play if you don't speak the language?" We endured, and finally Father picked us up. My friends and I liked to sit up in the balcony at the Kursaal and had to get there early to get seats in the front row. It was a very popular place. One day our favorite seats were occupied by a young man who reserved them by placing a magazine and a bag of toffees on each one while he went out to do something. Well, I helped myself to his toffees and my friends said, "If you, why not us?" We left only one candy at the bottom of the bag, and even took his magazine! When he returned, he was furious. The boys who were with us, no doubt wanting to show off, threatened to beat him if he didn't stop harassing us, which brought to mind an Arabic proverb that had us in stitches when I teased and told it. It was "*Darabni we-baka, we saba'ni we-shtaka,*" which means that the culprit instead of the victim was the one to rush into fits of weeping and lamenting to cover up his misconduct and make all believe he had been wronged. Of course, the culprit was me!

My grandfather Aslan lived in Khartoum, where he had a thriving gum business. Gum arabic was collected from the *Acacia nilotica* and exported for many uses. I knew it as an ingredient in a special kind of ice cream called *Gelati bi-l-mistika* (ice cream with gum). It was stretchy, resin flavored, and delicious. Our second-favorite ice cream, a tricolored slab, was Italian cassata, which we went to the posh downtown café called Groppi to eat on special occasions. Ice cream was a summer-only treat, never available at any other time. We could not imagine ice cream in winter until we came to the United States.

Nena Sara lived and raised my mother and Tante Yvette in Sudan. But after Salma and Yvette married men who lived in Egypt, she moved to Cairo to be near her daughters, bringing with her a servant girl named Adiba and a boy named Amin. They were, as children, initially sold as slaves to my grandfather and freed by him as he abhorred the institution of slavery. Adiba and Amin stayed in the family as paid household servants until they died. Mother and Tante Yvette's marriages to Aharon, my father, and Elam, my uncle, were arranged through a matchmaker. Mother was sixteen and Tante Yvette fifteen. Uncle Elam we always called Oncle 'Asfur (Uncle Bird) because he liked to sing and was, in fact, a cantor at Shaar ha-Shamayim, the Gates of Heaven Synagogue.

Grandfather continued to live in Sudan until his death, and took a boat and train to travel to Cairo to visit us. That railway line was built by the British from Cairo to Khartoum. Originally used for military transport, it made access to Sudan easier and opened up trade routes for many like my grandfather. My grandfather's business flourished and he helped fund a synagogue and a Jewish social club in Khartoum. I was heartbroken when I heard that that synagogue had been demolished in the 1980s and the Jewish cemetery desecrated.

But let me get back to childhood memories and happier times.

I remember Grandfather vividly on these visits, as he always brought us presents and his pockets always jingled with coins. When he went down for a nap, he draped his trousers over a chair and all the coins fell out. I used to sneak into his room and gather them up. When I had enough, I'd run to the corner store and buy candy. I was not about to return this bounty—certainly not!

I remember a story my mother told frequently. It had to do with my eyes. A neighbor came to visit her shortly after I was born. This woman was evidently known for her kindness, and for this reason everyone called her Umm al-Khayr, meaning Mother of Kindness or Mother of Good Tidings. Umm al-Khayr asked my mother, "Do you want your daughter's eyes to be strong and healthy?" Mother replied, "Yes, of course." So she recommended that Mother apply compresses soaked in warm water and onion juice to my eyes, adding, "When she is seven days old, apply kohl mixed with onion juice to the rims of her eyelids. This will keep her eyes healthy and bright." My mother took the advice to heart and I enjoyed healthy eyes throughout childhood and even today have uncommonly good eyesight. When we studied the history of ancient Egypt in school, I learned that Egyptian women used kohl throughout the ages, this same sulfide of antimony we use today to protect eyes and enhance their beauty. Did Umm al-Khayr possess this ancestral knowledge? Was it passed down from one generation of women to another? Even little boys had kohl put in their eyes as babies to protect them and perhaps also to keep out the sun's glare. Women use kohl to this day throughout the Middle East and I do too. But need I tell you that I avoid the onion juice?

Like my father's family, my mother's family was originally from Iraq. She had a brother who died in infancy before her family left Iraq for Sudan when Mother was a babe in arms. Tante Yvette was born in Sudan a year later. My father, like my mother, was born in Iraq but lived there until the age of eighteen, when he traveled to Egypt alone. Iraq had a significant Jewish community before 1950, a strong community. Father proudly reminded us that the Talmud had been compiled in the land of his birth, which was called Babylonia before it became Iraq. He said that Iraqi Jews considered themselves Arabs of Jewish faith until discrimination in the 1930s caused many to leave for Egypt, Sudan, and eventually to Palestine when the state of Israel was established as a homeland for the Jews. My father claimed that in his case, however, he left for Egypt not to flee persecution, but to seek his fortune, and because of a family conflict.

He told this story: "I was the middle child in a family of three brothers and one sister. My father was a businessman who died while I was a toddler and I do not remember him. My mother, Esther, raised us on the income from properties that Father left, but lost them all to her brothers when she fell ill and was too vulnerable to protect herself from their greed. There was a plague epidemic at the end of the nineteenth century, and when my sister succumbed and died, Mother was grief-stricken. She became so depressed and couldn't get out of bed for a long time. Her brothers said they would take care of her by running her affairs. In fact, they took advantage of her, stealing her assets and her money. How? They paid a woman to impersonate her and sign over her properties to them. Mother was now not only heartbroken, but broke. She struggled with the little her brothers gave her, helpless to do anything about their betrayal. I was old enough to understand but also could do nothing. However, I vowed to leave Iraq as soon as I could, and to seek my fortune in Egypt, where I had an uncle, my father's brother. I told Mother I would send for her and my youngest brother as soon as I could. And I did. My oldest brother was a rabbi and remained in Iraq to tend to his community. Mother embraced me with tears running down her cheeks the day I left. I was eighteen. After I established myself, I sought a wife, married, and soon after brought my mother and brother from Iraq and we made a good life in Egypt."

My father arrived in Egypt in a time of plenty, when all kinds of people were welcomed to her shores. There was a lot of opportunity for business. Father started to work with his uncle, the first member of Father's family to immigrate. Great-uncle Salama, my paternal grandfather's youngest brother, was in the textile business. He helped my father get started, sheltering him and showing him the ropes. A few years later, my father went into wholesale on his own, making bedsheets. I remember him saying something about Cartoni, an Italian firm with whom he first did business.

Nena Sara, as I said, lived with us. When Nena Esther came, she also lived with us, but soon after her younger son, Abraham, married Rachma, she was sent to live with him. However, Rachma could not stand her mother-in-law and he soon sent her back to us. Now both grandmothers lived with us. Our household consisted of Mother, Father, two grandmothers, three daughters, one son, and the servants Adiba and Amin. The grandmothers shared a room. Of course, our parents had their own room. We three girls had the biggest bedroom. Another room was a windowless cubicle, originally intended as a storage room. This space was fitted out with a privacy curtain and a cot for Adiba. It had no door. Our brother, who was the youngest, had a very small room, which was originally intended as a utility or sewing room. We had one large bathroom and the actual toilet was in a cubicle of its own, off to the side. Amin slept in a room on *al-setuh* (the rooftop), along with other servants and our washing tubs. With so many people in one apartment, frictions mounted. To satisfy Mother, to avoid conflicts he could not resolve, and to keep some semblance of peace at home, my father rented a room in the home of another Jewish family for his own mother, who became a boarder. When Nena Esther died there, he was wracked with guilt. It was heartbreaking to hear his sobs and the words he spoke: "I took in my wife's mother, but left my own to die among strangers!"

Our family was fairly traditional but not orthodox. I didn't really feel different from my friends because of being Jewish. We were Jews, Christians, and Muslim girls at Mère de Dieu, the Catholic school I attended. I envied the Catholic girls wearing pretty white dresses for first communion, but all in all our religion did not interfere with our friend-ships. My best friends were Mariam, who was Coptic; Athena, who was Greek, and Suheir, who was Muslim, as well as Adina and Aline, two other Jewish girls. I have a feeling we were far more relaxed about religion in the 1930s and 1940s than people generally are today. The Coptic friends I have kept in touch with tell me that their children now raise their own children pretty close to the church and that they tend to socialize exclusively within their church community. This was not so in my time. Of course, my fam-ily followed Jewish traditions to some extent: We celebrated the feasts, my father said the after-meal prayer in Hebrew, and we went to synagogue on special occasions. Mother sent our lunches to school in nesting containers carried by Amin—usually rice, vegetables, and a meat dish. At home, she was fairly open-minded about certain dietary restrictions, however, allow-ing us to eat pork because we liked it, and she purchased it from time to time at the Christian butchery. We liked cold cuts like mortadella and she let us have them at home, but never touched pork herself and warned: "Eat directly from the paper and don't ever put pork on our plates!" As we got older, she became more conservative and told us that she would never eat a meal at our houses after we married because she could not be sure any of the six of us children would keep a kosher house. Mother died suddenly of a heart attack shortly after my oldest sister, Abigail, married, and sadly we were not given a chance to test her resolve. She is buried in the cemetery at Basatin, one of the largest Jewish cemeteries in the world, the land for which was given in AD 400 by Egypt to the Jewish community. This cemetery reflected the size of the community, which grew to around eighty thousand, until it dwindled to a handful of Jews after the main exodus in the late 1940s and 1950s. As you see, not all of the Jews left Egypt with Moses!

Other than telling us about the Iraqi origins of the Talmud, my father did not speak to us of religion and I don't believe it played a central part in his life, not really. The night Mother died was a Friday, and he was at the coffeehouse socializing and playing backgammon with his friends. We had observed the Shabbat, and instead of spending the rest of the evening with family, he walked over to the coffeehouse. Evidently, he did not have a problem with that. Father always said, "I am Egyptian and my language is Arabic." In fact, when given a choice to be a British subject or an Egyptian around 1917, he chose the latter. He did not have a passport and I don't know how he traveled initially from Iraq to Egypt, but once in Egypt, he chose to carry an Ottoman *laissez-passer*, a document issued by the government of Egypt allowing travel. *Laissez-passer* is French for "allow passage," that is, to permit travel across borders. Many Iraqi Jews had these, especially after Operation Ezra and Operation Nehemiah in the early 1950s, when Jewish citizens were told they could leave Iraq safely on condition of renouncing their citizenship and turning over their properties and assets. Discrimination had become rampant, and fearing for their lives, Jews left in droves. Over one-hundred thousand Jews left their Iraqi homeland at that time, I think, although this was not the case for my father, who left Iraq before World War I.

Father wore a *tarboosh* (fez), buying a hat only when business finally took him to Europe. Other than that, he wore Western clothes—a suit and tie. Every morning, while drinking his coffee, he read the Arabic newspapers. He said that Arabic was his mother tongue, and the one he preferred to use. He kept his books and business ledgers in Arabic and wanted my mother to keep household accounts in the same way. She refused to keep books in any language, saying that when she needed money, she would just ask him for it. She had no other source of income.

As our families prospered, Father sought richer surroundings and lifestyles, deciding to move us from the middle-class neighborhood of Daher to a pair of luxurious apartments downtown, on Suleiman Pasha Street. Both families moved into the same building. Unlike today's Egypt where, I'm told, apartments are almost impossible to find, when I was a child they were readily available and rents were cheap. In fact, landlords offered promotions: one month free to move in.

Soon after we moved downtown, to Suleiman Pasha Street, Father persuaded my uncle to take a look at a villa in Helwan, a town south of Cairo. They decided to rent together. Our families shared this weekend retreat away from the city, where we enjoyed pure air and mineral-water springs said to fortify and cure any ailment under the sun. Mother loved it. She made sure to pack up the family and spend a few days of rest and relaxation there every few weeks. We arrived, unpacked, and went directly to the springs while Adiba and Amin prepared beds, shopped, cooked, and served meals on the wide veranda overlooking the Nile. Father and Mother encouraged us all to "sniff" the good air and "take" the cure, drinking glass after glass of the mineral waters and soaking daily in the mineral springs. I still have the glass I used there. Each one of us had a glass specifically meant for use in Helwan.

There was an astronomical observatory in Helwan, the Khedivial Astronomical Observatory, built in the early 1900s. It was from there that scientists observed Halley's Comet. I'm not sure why this detail comes to mind, unless it is because I loved watching stars and that, remembering Helwan, I am also remembering the nights spent there. There were few lights, the nights were dark and clear, the stars bright and beautiful. I called them "sky jewels." Did we go to the Khedivial Observatory? Oddly, I don't remember.

Like any man in business, my father had ups and downs, of course. Mother was careful. After Adiba and Amin died, no servants lived in again, but Mother hired servants to replace them as day helpers. In lean years, these women were the first to go to save money. By and large, however, Father's business flourished, as did that of Uncle Elam, who had started out selling rugs door-to-door, then imported tea to sell in Egypt, and eventually invested in real estate and became quite wealthy. Tante Yvette and Uncle Elam were richer than we were, and she began to hire maids from abroad, women from Italy and Yugoslavia. They were a status symbol and were often exploited. I remember Uncle Elam saying that he did not like it when his daughters showed off and boasted about their wealth. This was in part because, hearing them and seeing their riches, these foreign maids then demanded more money.

Neither Uncle Elam nor my father ever forgot how they had come up in the world. They contributed to Jewish charities like La Goutte de Lait (the drop of milk), an orphanage founded by the Benarroios in 1917 and located on Qasr al-Nil Street. La Goutte de Lait not only took in orphans, but children of poor families, giving them an excellent education, food, and clothing, and even supporting their *Bar Mitzvahs*. My sister Abigail's husband, Adlai, whose father had died and left the family destitute, was raised at La Goutte de Lait and made a success of himself working for the Cairo Motor Company, selling cars. A British national founded that company, sold British cars, and also earned a franchise to sell Ford motorcars in Egypt and Sudan. Abigail's husband, who was passionate about soccer, played the game and coached teams in his free time. I remember that he took his players to the Parisiana Café and the St. James Restaurant when they won games. The Parisiana was near the Cinema Diana and the St. James near Emad al-Din Street. When the Cairo Motor Company burned down during the 1952 revolution, its owners left Egypt. Soon after, Abigail and her family also left, making their new home in Israel.

As I matured, I became more and more interested in boys. There was an office building across from our apartment building. Seeing a young man standing on a balcony, I turned to my sister and exclaimed, "How handsome he is!" I watched for him after that, calling him *"Le beau des beaux,"* the handsomest man of them all. What a romantic I was! When I actually met him a few years later, I was stunned to see that, not only was he not the handsomest of them all, but he was downright ugly. As an impressionable and sheltered teenager, the fact alone that he was male caused me to think of him as handsome. Of course, I liked the company of boys, and our friends, boys and girls, came to the house or we went to the houses of the children whose families our parents knew. There was no such thing as dating. We went out in groups.

At home, we lived much as other middle-class Egyptian families did. We ate much the same food, except perhaps for sofrito for the Sabbath meal. Some families prepared it with lamb or veal, but Mother preferred chicken, which she braised in oil and a small amount of water, adding lemon, cardamom, and turmeric. This dish cooked very slowly, and toward the end, Mother added cubed potatoes that she had deep fried. If she did make sofrito with veal, she didn't add much to it because Egyptian veal was so flavorful. She simply cut up the meat, sautéed it, added a little water, salt, pepper, and cardamom, and let it cook very slowly. If she made it with beef, no cardamom was added. From time to time, she cooked a fish sofrito, and in this case stewed it with salt, pepper, and cumin. We also used cumin to flavor meatballs and ground lean beef at home, using a little oil to cook it in. We had to have rice at every meal. Father insisted on it. He even ate rice with salad, but as he rarely came home for lunch, Mother sent Amin with it to the shop in Hamzawi. On Fridays, we ate together and the meal usually included chicken in some form and chicken soup. Lunch was served at one o'clock and dinner around eight. Dinner was something light, and in winter we always had vegetable or lentil soup.

Sporting clubs were not really part of our social life as we were growing up, although they became so for the generation that came after us. I became a member of the sporting clubs in Cairo after I married because my husband was involved in sports. There was the Heliopolis Sporting Club, the Maadi Sporting Club, and the Tawfiqiya Club, which was smaller and more accessible to members of the middle class than the other two, which tended to be more upper class. Did you know that Maadi was founded by members of the Mosseri family, Egyptian Jews? It traces its history to the early 1900s, when the railroad was built between Cairo to the north and Helwan to the south. In Zamalek, the Gezira Sporting Club, which was only open to Egyptians after the British were ousted in 1956, was where I went to have lunch as a guest of a group of Coptic and Muslim friends, former schoolmates, all of whom lived in Zamalek. We played cards, chatting about everything and nothing. I continued to meet them there until 1960, a year before we left Egypt by choice. My father and mother had died and there was no one left to keep us attached to this country, which had grown hostile to the Jews and other minority communities. We were considered Egyptianized Jews, Mutamassirin, and when the time came to leave, we were made to sign a declaration that we were leaving of our own free will and relinquishing all of our assets to the Egyptian government. This was a sad, sad day for us!

But let me get back to my father for a moment.

Father had a weakness for fine china and refused to eat on anything but porcelain plates. As his shop was near a porcelain wholesaler, he often brought home sets of plates and cups that were remaindered. We had quite a few sets at home, as well as Christofle tableware, which I sent to my brother in Paris. He had left some years before we did, saying, "I never want to see the face of Egypt ever again!" He was angry and his heart never softened toward the country of his birth.

But to return to our house . . . Our house was furnished more for comfort than to follow a particular style or fashion, but as Father was an amateur collector of beautiful objects, he brought home from his travels such things as a Murano glass chandelier and a very large Venetian mirror. We had a rosewood curio cabinet, which we called a 'vitrina'—a vitrine in which crystal goblets and stem glasses were kept, to which Father added periodically. Over the years, the vitrina became so laden with glassware that it literally creaked. One day, as we were cleaning it before one of the holidays, it toppled over and much of the contents was broken. What pieces remained, we eventually sold after Father died. Rivoli, a fine department store in downtown Cairo, willingly bought them in matching pairs. As for the furniture, we auctioned it. Whatever else was left at the time of our exodus was confiscated.

In our family, as in so many other middle-class families, wasting food was thought to be a sin. We were told to look at the poverty around us and not waste. This habit stood us all in good stead during the lean years following our exodus.

At home, in Cairo, nothing was thrown away. If we had a party, we sent leftovers down to the doorkeeper, the *bawwab* and his family. We took stale bread to the chicken merchant for his chickens, as at the time chickens were sold live, not cleaned and packaged as in the supermarkets here. I still carry over one of our customs by drying my old bread in the oven, keeping it crisp in a tin box as Mother used to do. I enjoy it with soup. I also enjoy using it to scoop up dips like tahini, or feta-cheese and yogurt, which I make at home and always keep on hand. I whip up a batch with olive oil, lime juice, salt, garlic, and dried mint, and keep it in a container in my refrigerator. My late husband loved it, and we sometimes had it with romaine lettuce and a few other nibbles with a glass of wine for dinner if we did not feel like cooking or going out. Even after moving to the United States, as in Egypt, our main meal was lunch. Dinner was nosh. Since in New York it is not done to send leftovers down to a doorman as we used to do in Cairo, I send cookies or a cake to him, saying, "You might enjoy this with your coffee, Arthur." He appreciates the gesture and the tip that sometimes is included along with the cookies. Old habits die hard. And besides, you know yourself that we all may have left Egypt under differing circumstances, but somehow Egypt has stayed with us in our habits, our comfort foods, our customs, how we interact with others. I have not shed the depth of feeling I have for Egypt, nor the nostalgia that comes over me like sweet and bitter scents from the past. *"Adi al-dunya be-helwaha wa-murraha"* (So it is with the world, its sweetness and bitterness intermingling).

When I think of Egypt, I think of Umm Kulthum, my father's favorite singer. Even though I am better acquainted with Western music, I have some recordings of "the Lady," as she was affectionately named. I play them on occasion. "Daret al-ayyam" (The days have rolled by, time's turning, turning) takes me back. I am transported to another time, which now lives only in *zakar*, remembrance.

4

Mimi

Meeting Mimi

I met Mimi at a dinner held by one of the members of the Jewish community I had befriended. She was visiting from Paris and actually looked very French in her perfectly tailored dinner suit, her pearls twined with antique beads, which I later found out she collected, designing and making the necklaces herself. She was tall and slender, her eyes slightly upturned, her small 'Parisian' nose perfectly powdered and a trace of pink on her lips. There was something feline about Mimi. Her smile was friendly yet discreet, her hands small and neat, nails buffed with no polish. She had fine blonde hair, worn in a French twist into which she had fixed a narrow silver comb. "Stylish," I thought when we were introduced. "Interesting," I thought after our first conversation. I made a mental note to ask her if she might have time during her visit to New York to meet with me, and if she would allow me to record her memories of Egypt. She was hesitant, but agreed when she found out that some of her friends were participating in this oral-history project. She was exceptional among this group, as she had learned and spoke Arabic. She had also done a lot of volunteer work in Egypt, and in so doing had interacted with a variety of needy women and children. As a result, she had gained a depth of experience members of her privileged class often lacked. I was eager to record her story.

I soon found out that she was a woman of few words, but spoke vividly, as you shall see.

Mimi tells her story

In the early part of the twentieth century, my parents, Chaim and Ana, left their native Russia on board a ship bound for South America. They had signed on with the Jewish Colonization Association, an organization created in 1891 by Baron Maurice de Hirsch, a German Jewish financier and philanthropist who dedicated himself and his resources to improving the lives of oppressed Jews living in Asia, Europe, and Russia. My parents were among this group. The association offered opportunities to thousands, safely removing them from homelands where they were increasingly at risk, facing ever-increasing restrictions, persecution, and death.

I did some research about the association and found the charter in which their stated goal was to "assist and promote the emigration of Jews from any parts of Europe or Asia, and principally from countries in which they may for the time being be subjected to any special taxes or political or other disabilities, to any other parts of the world, and to form and establish colonies in various parts of North and South America and other countries for agricultural, commercial, and other purposes."

When Baron de Hirsch died in 1896, the organization continued to aid Jews under the direction of his widow, Clara, and other like-minded philanthropists. The safe removal of Jews was still taking place without resistance from government authorities.

Chaim and Ana were newlyweds when they emigrated. They boarded a ship bound for Argentina, joining countless other Jews bound for South America to form agricultural colonies on that vast and lush continent. They never made it. Instead, they disembarked in Alexandria, one of the ship's ports of call. My mother often said when recounting this story, "*L'homme propose et Dieu dispose*" (Despite our best-laid plans, we end up where God wills). Ana fell ill on board ship, which is why my parents decided to cut their journey short and stay in Egypt. During their layover in Alexandria, they disembarked as transit passengers, while a helpful member of the crew, in whom they had confided, secretly carried their bags to them. When the ship sailed, it was minus two of its passengers. My parents said, "We never looked back."

As a result of complications from her illness, Mother could not easily conceive. When she finally became pregnant with me, a few years after arriving in Alexandria, she had a hard labor that left her unable to have more children. I was an only child, unusual in Jewish families at the time. My friends were all from families of no less than three children, and sometimes as many as fourteen. Mother said that I had been a longed-for, long-awaited gift, which is why they called me Miriam, the name of the Prophet Moses's sister as it appears in the Book of Exodus. It means "wished-for child."

As an only child, I had my parents' full, undivided attention. I sometimes missed having siblings, but not too much. When I was finally sent to the Jewish school and later to the Lycée Français, I enjoyed being with kids my age. I left school early to marry. Mother believed that marriage and motherhood were a woman's chief mission and greatest joy. So, acting on her convictions and conspiring to make a match between me and a friend's son, she introduced me to Avram. We liked each other right away and a year later Mother's friend became my mother-in-law. I was fifteen when I met Avram and sixteen when we married. He was twenty-six. We had our first child when I was eighteen, followed by two more.

Avram came to Egypt with his brothers when he was eighteen, all emigrating from Romania to escape persecution. They were seeking opportunities and hoping for a more pleasant life. "Jews," Avram said, "are ill-treated in Romania."

Unlike so many Jews and other foreigners living in Egypt at the time, my husband and his brothers learned Arabic and took Egyptian citizenship. They went into business together and established a successful button factory where all sorts of buttons were fabricated. They hired Egyptian workers and made fancy buttons for women's coats and dresses, shirt buttons, and buttons for military uniforms and other uniforms. If there was a niche for a certain button, Avram and his brothers filled it, eventually exporting their products. They prospered and our families were the beneficiaries of their success.

Avram and I had a very pleasant life in Egypt, a very comfortable life. There was an ease to Egyptian life in those days, the likes of which I have not experienced elsewhere, nor since. People were warm and friendly, jovial, welcoming. We integrated with ease into Egyptian life and made Egyptian friends, which was not typical of other Europeans, who by and large socialized with others of their communities.

In Alexandria, Avram and I had charming friends. A group of us went out together regularly and met at each other's homes, or packed picnics and drinks and went to the beach, where we had what we called cabins. They were cabanas you used when at the beach for a day or an evening, furnished with canvas chairs and, on some, canvas curtains for protection from the sun on hot days. Ours was on Stanley Beach. It was delightful. We savored every moment and our lives were relaxed and easy. I remember a lot of laughter and good times.

At home, we spoke Yiddish. We knew French and English, and learned Arabic, too. People in Egypt tended to be polyglots and we were no different. Some of our friends spoke Italian and German, too, but few learned Arabic.

Learning Arabic was Father's idea. He was unusual among Europeans living in Egypt, who most often turned their noses up at Arabic as the language of inferiors. What snobs! Arabic is a beautiful language, full of nuance, which Father appreciated and shared with me. Arabic was not taught in the schools I attended so Father hired a sheikh (Muslim cleric) to teach me at home. I did the same when my children started school and they are the richer for it. Now, in their professional lives, they can interact and do business successfully in the Arabic-speaking world. I refreshed my own language skills by sitting in on their lessons and enjoyed improving my written Arabic, too.

We led a life of ease, which meant that our children, like others of our circle of friends, were raised not only by us, but by nannies from Yugoslavia or from Gorizia, a village on the borders of Italy and Austria. This meant that I was free to come and go as I pleased. The children were taken care of, cleaning was done by an Egyptian maid, meals were prepared by our Nubian cook, and our meals were served by a butler in our service, a *sufragi*. So, really, everything was done for me. I simply organized and gave direction, and my household ran like clockwork.

I have always loved languages and enjoyed attending classes at various cultural centers promoting the language and culture of different countries. Remember that Alexandria was a very cosmopolitan city and hosted Greeks, Austrians, Swedes, and Jews from every part of the world. These cultural centers promoted the cultures of their nations, hosted art exhibits, and provided classes—especially language classes. I explored them all and enjoyed learning. It was my way of making up for not completing my high school education, and a nice way to meet new friends.

Every year, as a family, we took trips to Italy, to France, to Spain, traveling on excellent Italian liners such as the *Tristino* and the *Champollion*. My language skills were useful when traveling and also in Alexandria, a cosmopolitan city where all manner of languages were spoken, where many ethnic groups met and socialized. Life was beautiful.

We belonged to a number of clubs in Alexandria. We were members of the Sporting Club, the Royal Yacht Club, the club at Ras al-Tin. At some point Jews had been barred entry into these clubs. Then one day we got letters saying to disregard this order. I went to see Rabbi Nahum about the matter, to get his advice on what to do. He was the brilliant head of our community at the time, and in response to my consternation he said, "If you live in Egypt, you should enjoy everything that Egypt has to offer like any Egyptian would." I said, "If you say so, Rabbi, then I will do what you tell me to do and apply for membership at the clubs." He was blind by then, poor man. But what culture, what a memory he had!

Avram died of a heart attack when we were in the midst of our happiest and most productive years. I was devastated and could hardly get out of bed. Family and friends offered what support they could and, after a year of mourning, suggested I do volunteer work to fill the void. I pulled myself together, shed my black dresses, and went about the business of healing by helping others and by filling my time with charity work, or what we then called "good works."

My first efforts were on behalf of children, eventually focusing on a day-care center for Jewish children. We accepted only Jewish children because we taught them prayers and did not wish to come under government scrutiny as 'missionaries.' We did, however, establish a program called "Tadreeb al-Ummahat" (training of mothers), where we taught women of all faiths to sew, embroider, and cook. I raised money for this program and the Egyptian government matched it. We bought sewing machines with these funds and donated some each year to women who excelled in their work. The women were motivated to put forth their best efforts in hopes of getting a machine to take home. Some became seamstresses and supported their families by sewing for others.

Our Jewish elders also needed assistance and I put my best foot forward for them as well, spending time with old people who lived in a Jewish home for the elderly, funded by the Jewish community. It was a kosher home and therefore accepted only Jews. I was better suited to work with children and young mothers, however, and offered my time to another home for children in Cairo, L'Enfance Heureuse (Happy Childhood). I participated in a program that gave poor children from neighborhoods like Harat al-Yahud (the Jewish Quarter) a month-long vacation in Alexandria, a chance to enjoy fresh air, good food, and healthy activities, which included day-long excursions to different beaches. The community had purchased a spacious villa at Sidi Bishr, where groups of children were housed all summer long. The children were clothed and fed, coddled and cared for by paid staff and volunteers before being returned home to Cairo, their cheeks glowing with health. My participation in this program was very satisfying to me and filled me with hope for the future of these children.

My own children never experienced deprivation. Rather, they lived in comfort among other privileged children. My daughters were educated in French schools, and my son at Victoria College, a British school. When the Germans reached the gates of Alexandria, Alamein, I feared for my children. We were aware of the turmoil in Europe, though not fully aware of the extent of the horrors they were perpetrating. The Germans did not last long, however, and we breathed a sigh of relief. Still, they did make a positive impact with their cultural center, the Goethe Institute. In addition to my volunteering, I attended cultural programs there and learned some German. I was a widow, and it was a way to keep busy since my brothers-in-law took care of the family business and I had no hand in running it.

After the Egyptian revolution, and not long after the ousting of King Faruq, the family business was sequestered. Many businesses were taken by the government and the owners had to work there as employees. My son was an employee in his own father's factory, the business Avram had built with his vision and efforts. He was constantly under scrutiny, made to feel like a stranger in his own home.

The Jews passed through some difficult times after the revolution of 1952, which was a coup carried out by a group of Egyptian army officers. I suspect the United States had a hand in it, expecting the officers to be pro-American. They were not. We all suffered at that time and nothing was ever the same.

My family and I were not ourselves in any way involved in politics, but on certain national holidays we made small packets of buttons and candies that we donated for the government to distribute to people celebrating in the parks. Sham al-Nessim (the first day of spring) was one such holiday. Additionally, we gave an average of 10 percent of our profits to charities. In the 1940s, during the war years, we gave a portion of our earnings to hospitals.

Our goodwill did not earn us merits. Our lives gradually became more difficult in the 1950s and we felt a lot of hostility from people who once had been friendly. The servants became uppity as they drank in the words of Gamal Abd al-Nasser shouting about exploitation. My chauffeur married a maid, who hired a maid to carry her umbrella to the beach. It was ludicrous really. The cook wanted a gofer to help him. Many of our humble and devoted servants took liberties they would not have before the revolution. One said to me one day, "The way you live is wrong, Madame. It's wrong!" We had to adapt. I repeated, "This is my new life," and devised ways of shielding myself and my family from the ill will growing around us, focusing on the positives. Obstacles, slurs, and violence increased until life became almost intolerable. This was experienced even more so by the needy in our community. Those of us who could help, helped. The Jewish community had to take care of its own. Eventually, it dwindled and those left behind suffered greatly.

I would like to say a few more words about L'Enfance Heureuse, which was founded to aid working mothers who brought their children to the day-care center at eight and picked them up at five. We fed, clothed, and educated these children, and bathed them three times a week. This service gave mothers a chance to go out and make a living. Some had no means of support other than going to work. While they were at work, we took care of the children, offering them different nourishing meals and teaching them basic hygiene. In the morning, we served them *café au lait* (milk with a little coffee added), bread and milk, or bread and chocolate. At noon, lunch was a good, hot soup made with meat and barley, rice and lentils, okra and meat. Fruit was always plentiful, and rice pudding was a favorite dessert with the children. After lunch, the little ones napped in tiny beds constructed especially for the center. Clean sheets and blankets were provided, and the children were taught to fold them neatly on their beds. When we woke them, we showed them how to properly wash their hands and faces with soap and water, handing them each a towel of their own. Before their mothers returned to collect them, we fed them a snack of milk and tea, or plain milk cut with a little water. Why? Because Egyptian buffalo milk was heavy. A milkman delivered it to the center and helpers boiled it, letting it cool before serving it to the children, sometimes adding a little sugar. There was no such thing as pasteurized milk. We also served bread and jam daily with the milk.

This day-care center was of great service to mothers and children, some of whom needed a subsidy in order to attend. But mothers had to pay a minimal fee for the care of their children. We had noticed that it was not good to take the children for free and that paying something, however small, gave the mothers a sense of self-respect.

A few times a year we visited factories and asked for donations of fabric to sew clothes for the children, making little coats, dresses, shirts, pants, anything they needed. People gave readily to help keep the center going and care for these children. There were those who contributed goods, while others gave their time and assistance in person. Shoe factories gave shoes and sandals, and doctors gave vitamins and medicines, as the need was great. Our goal was to help mothers and also to provide a firm base on which children could grow and build their lives.

In the 1940s, people began to leave in droves. They either left or were ousted; some, like my parents, died without having to experience a hostile Egypt. Finally, no one remained. People went to Europe, to South America, to Israel, to the United States, to Australia. The Jews traveled and scattered to the four corners of the earth. Those who went to Israel had a difficult time, because there was constant conflict with the Arab population and it escalated despite peace talks and negotiations.

I became a Zionist when I felt the sting of discrimination and anti-Semitism growing around us. I started attending lectures and I listened. Always, I listened. I was not a Zionist because I was against Egypt, but Egypt grew angry with us and many of us began to look for ways to channel our energies and find safe havens for our people.

I cannot tell you how different life was when my parents established themselves in Alexandria. Egypt was heaven on earth and the Jews felt safe and prospered. Egyptians were well disposed toward the Jews until the 1940s. I'll never forget how the governor of Alexandria welcomed those fleeing persecution in other countries. He directed us, the Jewish community, to meet boats full of Jewish children, survivors of the Holocaust, to show them compassion and to help in whatever way we could.

He said, "Go meet the boats. Take food, candies, toys, pastries. Take everything they need to them. We will help." That's how it was, but not for long.

I will never forget the child who held up a bar of soap to show me and said, "This is my father and mother." They had been killed in the extermination camps, their bodies made into soap. This was a level of violence we did not experience in Egypt, though we gradually felt the winds of change.

There began to be arrests, especially of Zionists and leftists. It was a harsh reality we were facing, but nothing like Europe.

In the 1940s and 1950s people left in droves. Some were expelled. In Britain, Jewish refugees got subsidies to help them get started, and therefore Britain was a prize destination. Those who had British nationalities got 10,000 British pounds, the equivalent then of some $40,000.

Throughout history, the Jews have suffered. I would say that most of us are resilient and succeed wherever we make new homes. We have been adapting for a thousand years, haven't we?

Our love of Arabic, our love of Egypt, did not spare us the indignities we suffered in our last days in Egypt. We hung on until 1960, but the writing was on the wall. When we departed, our exit visas (visas required to leave even though we were unwanted) were stamped "*bidun rugu*" (return is forbidden). Our presence was unwanted, our hearts were heavy, yet we took the best of Egypt with us. Governments come and go, but Egypt is eternal. While some of us eventually returned to visit, most did not wish to set foot on Egyptian soil ever again. We had tasted the desert's grit after the Nile Valley's bounty. So it is in life, and so it was with us.

We are a resilient people, we the Jews, and we start over and over again wherever destiny plants us. But let me tell you, Egypt is a state of mind for us, a place of reminiscence. We enter it with longing, with regret, with anger, with love and tenderness even. We have left its shores but Egypt lives in us and will continue to dwell in our memories.

5
Chaviva

Meeting Chaviva

Zabar's is a speciality food store founded by Louis and Lilian Zabar in 1934. It occupies a city block on the Upper West Side of Manhattan and is a New York institution. It stocks just about any specialty food you can think of, and much more. I went there one day in search of *basterma*, a spice-infused, air-dried beef tenderloin savored in the Middle East, often eaten with eggs. When I asked for it at the deli, the server said, "You mean pastrami?" Before I could utter a word, a small, plump, gray-haired woman standing beside me piped up, "Of course not! It's not at all the same!" The woman was Chaviva. Giving me a curious look, she proceeded to enlighten the deli man. Right away I noticed her very dark eyes under painted-on dark brows and turned to ask her where she was from, though her manner and rolled *r*'s had already given her away. She started speaking a mile a minute in what teachers call a playground voice, and a line of impatient shoppers was forming behind us. I gently steered her toward the coffee bar and, mugs in hand, we proceeded to get acquainted. She was born in Egypt, she told me, and had lived on a farm until her family moved to Cairo. Chaviva, doing most of the talking, mentioned that she knew other Egyptians and began to name a few, asking if I knew them too. Ester, whom I had already met, was one, so Chaviva suggested we get together. I was on board and already wondering about the story I would glean from her when we got to know each other better. She suggested we call Ester and make a date to go to Brooklyn for lunch at a Middle Eastern restaurant she liked and shop for *basterma* at Sahadi's, one of New York's best grocery stores, founded by Syrian migrants in the 1940s. I agreed and another New

York friendship was born. And yes, she did eventually tell me her story and agreed to let me record it.

Chaviva tells her story

I am Chaviva Botbol. My parents called me Viva as I was growing up, although I prefer now to be called Chaviva, my true name, which in Hebrew means 'beloved.' Not everyone can be persuaded to give up calling me Viva, but most have respected my wish. I can say that I was certainly the beloved of my parents, and their unconditional love gave me a strength I possess to this day.

My parents lived in the countryside and we, their children, were born at home with the help of a midwife. Several children before me died in infancy. My mother grieved for the lost babies, of course, but then went on to have three boys who survived, continuing to lead the busy life of a country wife. The Yiddish word *balabusta* (a good homemaker) describes my mother to a T. The only help she had running our home at the *'izba* (farm) was a peasant woman and her little daughter, who was more of an encumbrance than a help. Zubeida milked our *gamusa* (water buffalo) and set the milk aside to settle in a cool place in our pantry, which Mother called her *karar*, a Turkish word, I think. Within a few hours, a layer of cream rose to the top of the milk, thick enough to scoop onto a plate. We mixed it with honey or molasses for breakfast. Mother also made cheese, rolling it in a straw mat to make logs of feta, which she preserved in brine. Much of our food and clothing was homegrown and homemade. A neighbor tended our beehives and took part of the honey in return for his service. We led a typical country life, much like that of other landowners around us, Copts and Muslims.

Mother told me that, with each birth of a brother, she felt a twinge of regret at not having had a girl. She told me she thought about how a daughter would grow up and be a companion to her. She longed for this companionship. When I came along, she said she felt as if she had "sprouted wings of joy," adding, "You were a gift from God Chaviva, a gift to your old parents." I was their last child.

Some people want boys, some want girls, some want both, and some want none. As I said, I had three brothers who died and three who survived. Two were sent to the Alliance Israelite school in Alexandria and lived with Father's relatives during the school terms, coming home for holidays. The third was sent to France, to the Lycée Français in Marseille.

Monsieur Buret, a French friend of my parents and himself a teacher, said to them, "Eldad is very bright. He would benefit from an education in France. His chances here are limited. You should send him abroad. It would help him broaden his horizons." He was indeed the brightest of my three brothers. My parents took the teacher's advice and made arrangements for him to go to France.

Eldad, a Hebrew name, means "beloved of God." He was the brother I was closest to and I wept when he departed. Not for long, though, as you shall see. He was also the most beloved of our parents and sending him away was a sacrifice. He soon returned, however, too homesick to stay away. Eldad was so thin-skinned, he suffered terribly from the slights and ridicule leveled at him at school because he was small, and had prominent ears that embarrassed him and a large nose, which his tormentors called a Jewish nose, teasing him about it and about being a Jew with a "funny" name.

We Jews have always had to contend with discrimination. Between the wars, however, when Eldad was sent to France, the atmosphere went from unfriendly to deadly. It was a good thing he came back.

As for me, Mother wanted me by her side. Because of this, she was reluctant to send me to school, keeping me at home until the age of eight. I would happily have stayed near her, helping around the house and in the garden, collecting chicken eggs from the coops and playing with my pet chicken, Samra. I called her Samra, meaning dark, because she was almost black.

Though my mother had limited schooling, she was a very smart, practical woman and taught me many things. She taught me to read and do sums, to sew, which I liked very much, and to knit and embroider, which I did not care for as much. I loved drawing and painting, however, and Mother started me painting on leather and velvet. I created hangings and also painted on wood. One year, I painted three long panels, which a local carpenter turned into a trifold screen for our dining room. Two side panels for this paravent were decorated with fruits and vegetables. On the central panel I painted a little boy climbing a tree to "steal" mangoes. My little thief had a dog yapping at the base of the tree, pulling at his britches, tearing them and showing his tush. Such themes were very popular when I was growing up, as were these screens. Even now, despite arthritic fingers, I still paint on velvet and donate my work to raise money for a senior center to which I belong.

When I was sixteen, Avram and I were introduced. He was looking for a wife, and we liked each other right away and married a year later. He came from a Sephardic family who, like us, were cotton growers. My parents had a large home and we started married life under their roof.

My parents and brothers had all died by the time Egypt turned sour toward the Jews. We ourselves saw the writing on the wall in the 1950s, but held fast, hoping it would pass. It did not, and when our lands were sequestered and our means of livelihood impacted, we lost hope and began planning our exit, leaving for Israel in the 1960s. We stayed two years, then moved to New York, where we were sponsored by distant cousins. Life in Israel was too rugged after Egypt, but change is part of life. We adjusted as we went, and when asked how we were doing always said, "All is well."

My ancestors were from North Africa, but my parents were born and raised in Egypt, as were my grandparents. They owned land and we lived in a large, comfortable house on our farm, our *'izba*. We had such a healthy, peaceful, pleasant life. We loved it.

My father grew cotton. There were other Jewish families scattered about rural Egypt, but our own neighbors were mostly of the Muslim and Coptic faiths. They all loved my father, who was generous and kind to the peasants who worked his land. We had a huge garden and orchard, eating more vegetables and fruits than meat. It was so pleasant, so pleasant. We had houseguests all the time. During the summer, our teacher Monsieur Buret came with his family and stayed with us for a month. We had a huge house, but as we were kosher, we also had a guesthouse for non-Jewish visitors. We called it the *salamlik*. Life was easy, so easy!

The weather in Egypt was mild and dry. Our farm was beautiful and peaceful. The nearest city, Mansura on the Nile Delta, was where we went for major purchases. After my parents moved to Alexandria to join my brother, who had married there, my father went back and forth to supervise work on the *'izba* and to take care of business. He traveled by train, taking with him my brothers so they could one day step into his shoes. That day never came, as they did not care for country living, and eventually it would have made no difference anyway, as our lands were taken away from us. Eldad was the first to leave. He went to Paris and began to think of himself as a Frenchman. Sadly, he was killed in France at the time of the German invasion.

My husband went into the textile business with one of his uncles and prospered. Our circumstances improved such that we were able to build a beautiful villa in Smouha, where we enjoyed some good years before having to leave Egypt. We had many Jewish friends and we entertained a lot in Smouha. We had very nice Egyptian neighbors, and we were cordial and friendly until the end.

Every Sunday, one member of the family would host the rest for lunch. We made big meals, sweets, and all sorts of dishes. I was not a very good cook, and luckily was able to hire one who stayed with us until the day we left Egypt. Two of my children are better cooks than I am. My daughters Aliza and Anat have great culinary skills, and Ravi, my son, says, "Children make up for what their parents lack." He is probably right. He became a chef and lives in New York City.

We had such a comfortable life in Egypt. I lived like a queen. My friends came over. My family came over all the time. The house in Smouha was always full of people and we had a very pleasant time. Life was cheap, too, and everything was available, both local goods and imported goods. At least once a week I met my friends at Athineos or Pastroudis, elegant cafés in Alexandria. We had tea, pastries, chatted. I didn't have to do anything at home except organize and delegate. The servants shopped, cooked, cleaned, did the laundry, everything; all was taken care of. In the evening we socialized, played cards, had drinks with friends and family, or went to the movies. We also went to the theater to see the Comédie Française, which performed frequently in Egypt. We spent time in what were then called "Casinos," which were café-bars on the sea. Vendors peddled their wares on the sidewalks. We liked the one who came along with pistachios and played a game with him. We grabbed a handful of nuts and make a bet with Ali, the vendor, as to how many we had in each hand. If we guessed right, we kept them; if not, we paid him a piaster for each nut in our hands. It was fun. We had a lot of fun. Other vendors came along with cooked shrimp, which we bought to enjoy with Stella beer on summer nights. It was so very, very pleasant and lighthearted. Egyptians were so friendly. We laughed and laughed, told stories and jokes, and the word *lonely* never entered the vocabulary of this family!

We spoke French and Arabic at home. Our children studied at the British Boys' School and the English Girls' College. Hebrew prayers were taught and the boys were prepared for *Bar Mitzvah*. In Egypt, there was no such thing for girls; no *Bat Mitzvah* existed in our Sephardic tradition.

My parents were devout, but my husband was a freethinker, even though his father was devout and followed tradition to the letter. He used to say, "If you pull the rope too tight, it chokes." And so he left room for each to think as he pleased.

My husband sold Egyptian cotton to the United States and traveled there a lot. He always took me with him. We traveled on the *Queen Mary* and the *Queen Elizabeth*. When we went to Europe, we traveled on the *Esperia*, a beautiful Italian liner. We stayed at the nicest hotels and once brought back a new American car, a silver Buick. We led a beautiful life in Egypt. We had a good life here, too, but there was something about Egypt that inspired you to savor everything more. I cannot explain it.

There were years of sadness, of course, when loved ones died. There was hardship, too, when the cotton market crashed and my father was bankrupted. But we always bounced back, and were taught endurance. My spirit never failed me. I focused on joy, telling myself that if my thoughts were glad thoughts, not gloomy thoughts, I would live joyfully no matter what trials came my way, and no matter what I lost. When all is said and done, I'd say that the years of happiness and the years of prosperity were greater than the years of sadness and difficulty. We are fortunate.

Our greatest sadness came when we could not avoid the reality of a changing Egypt. We had lived in harmony with our neighbors until the mid-1940s, when we saw that Jews were beginning to suffer persecution. We hung on for two decades, hoping the climate would improve, but the hatred escalated. Jews were being arrested, mistreated, and their properties violated, seized, and confiscated. It was hard.

In 1960, we could no longer put our heads in the sand. We had to go. It was rough. We could not take any of our possessions with us. However, they could not take our memories away. We had had so many good years! Rebuilding our lives was difficult, but we were resilient and did it. After Israel, we took our growing family and moved to New York, where a cousin helped us get started again.

We lived so well in Egypt for so many years. We were like brothers and sisters with our Muslim and Christian neighbors. Our servants were devoted to us and we to them, and they served us well and made a good living. Everything was easy. Egypt had anything you could ever want: the climate was wonderful, the people warm and funny, the history fascinating, the food delicious, shopping was easy and goods were bountiful, and oh, the sunshine! In spite of the storms, I continue to believe that for those who plan peace there is joy.

As for Egypt, what can I say, what can I say? Once it is a part of you, it stays a part of you. I have discarded the thorns and kept the flowers.

6

Maaya

Meeting Maaya

The first time I laid eyes on Maaya was in New York City's East Village. While strolling up Second Avenue, I was intrigued by a sign that read Jivamukti Yoga Center. I had not heard of yoga, and was puzzling over what this place might be when a yogini on her way to class stopped and said hello. She explained about the center and declared cheerily, "Come up, come up! It's the best thing you will ever do for yourself." And indeed it was and has been ever since. The yogini, whom I soon called "my encourager," was Maaya.

She was an attractive senior, hair buzzed, tinted lavender, and shorter still around her ears, from which hung iridescent feathers. She was about five foot six, a trim figure clad in black tights, and a tank top with a rain-forest scene visible under her open, gray fleece jacket. Her dark eyes were rimmed with kohl, giving them depth and drama. Her milk-white skin was powdered a shade I thought I recognized. Aunt Lucienne, my mater-nal uncle's French wife, wore it. I remember the name: 'nacre,' mother of pearl. Slung over her left shoulder, Maaya carried a narrow black backpack stamped with a bold red Om symbol. A black yoga mat stuck out of the top. Her face was catlike, and her appearance striking. She was unforgettable, really, as was her story once I heard it.

After my initiation to yoga, Maaya invited me to attend satsang to chant, meditate, and hear spiritual discourse from various teachers. We began to attend together. I lived uptown and she in Gramercy Park. We often caught the same bus to the East Village, and in the course of one of those stop-and-go rides, Maaya told me about Ananda Ashram in Monroe, New York, founded in the 1960s by Sri Brahmananda Saraswati. She was a devotee of the great teacher and took me there for my first Thanksgiving retreat. "Attending satsang will bring you home to yourself," she used to say. When she told me her story, it was like another homecoming.

Maaya tells her story

I have always been interested in numerology and astrology, and found out from a book I read that the number five is associated with my name. Whether this is true or not, I liked the description of five as a dynamic and energetic number, signifying balance, non attachment, resourcefulness, and harmony. I strive for these qualities in my life. I believe in free will up to a point, and also in predestination up to a point. I seek out paths and guides that can help me grow, while believing that some of what happens to us happens for reasons. Obviously, some of what does happen cannot be changed, like being ousted from Egypt, which is the country of my birth. Destiny led the Jews out of Egypt more than once. I was witness to one such departure.

I was born in the coastal city of Alexandria in the spring of 1937, on the eve of terrible events in Europe. In Egypt, people still felt safe. I was the fourth child of Jewish parents who had expected to have no more children after me, as their first offspring did not survive. They took these losses to mean something was wrong with them. Was it karma?

When they had all but given up, my mother was surprised by her pregnancy, and when I arrived hale and hearty, they rejoiced. But there is more to this story than meets the eye. I will tell you in a moment. For now, suffice to say that I was not to be the last of their children. They had twins two years later, my brother Nessim and sister Daniella.

I have tried to reconstruct a scene unfurling in the summer of 1936, when my mother told my father what she thought would be welcome news, and was shocked that he took flight. They had a brief period of separation as my father, it seems, was afraid that this child too would not survive. But survive I did, and my father returned to hold me and to beg Mother's forgiveness.

The story goes that people rousted my father out and told him he must go home, that he now had a healthy daughter with a lusty voice. "This one's a survivor," they said. "You should hear her wail!" Until he returned, my mother refused to name me. And when he did they could not immediately agree on a name. My father, however, told me that when he gazed into my eyes, he saw fierce resolve and also recognition: "Where have we met before?"

As it turned out, over the years, my father and I bonded more than he did with any others in the family. My father believed that we had many lives and many incarnations, and that we had met in some previous life. He said, "When I saw you, Maaya, I felt an overwhelming sense of recognition, and when you looked back at me, I was sure ours was a reunion." He consulted a psychic, who told him that once upon a time I had been his teacher.

My father and I enjoyed a sense of ease together, maybe because we were a lot alike. As I grew up, he shared his interests with me. We had the same sense of curiosity and a desire to know things, and were both voracious readers. We became buddies and now I think that we were soul mates.

Father died suddenly during my last year of high school. I was devastated. To this day, I am my father's daughter, and I think that his expressed recognition of our connection through the ages, his devotion to nurturing my young mind and expanding my interests in areas beyond our community and traditions, served me well. He helped launch in me a curious and open mind, while his unconditional love helped me be strong and resilient. This is not to say that we always agreed, but the fabric of what we shared was strong and elastic, contributing to our enjoyment of each other's company even when we disagreed. His mentorship of me from the start was like a magical food that nourished me daily when he was alive and sustained me after he died.

My father was a history professor with a passion for Eastern religions and philosophies. He read widely, and he read to me starting from when I was a baby. The memory of his voice accompanies me to this day.

As a young man, my father had attended talks by a visiting Hindu spiritual leader. It was perhaps then that he learned about *Maya*, a Sanskrit word meaning illusion, and when I came along he wanted to pick my name from among the Hindu deities. My father occasionally let slip snippets of how he and Mother split up, how they got back together, how I got this name of mine. He said, "I wanted to name you Durga after an invincible goddess, but your mother said no. Thinking that you came to us like an apparition, a dream, an illusion, I then suggested Maaya. You were no illusion, but a dream come true. Mother refused both names and proposed Rebecca. It did not suit you, I thought. We went back and forth, and finally we found one we could both accept." Mother said, "We can call her Maaya, 'Spring' in Hebrew. Like spring, she brings us hope and a fresh start." That's close enough to Maya, my father thought. He agreed to Mother's choice, and this is how I became Maaya.

There was something ethereal about my father. He looked a little like the philosopher Krishnamurti and quoted him often. Since those long-ago days, I have carried with me one of Father's bookmarks. It is yellowed and dog-eared, but treasured. Using his ink pen he had copied this thought from Krishnamurti: "Tell your friend that in his death, a part of you dies and goes with him. Wherever he goes, you also go. He will not be alone." In my head I substituted "father" for "friend."

My mother was very different from my father. She was practical, energetic, not a dreamer. She was intelligent, but not an intellectual. What had attracted my father to her? Probably her beauty and vivacious nature. What had attracted her? Probably his good looks, his black, black eyes, and his gentle nature. I'm guessing that some part of my father felt undernourished in a marriage that provided him with none of the spiritual companionship he craved. When I came along, I filled a void. I was a kindred spirit.

From Father, I acquired curiosity, a thirst for learning, a love of reading, and a need for spirituality in my life. I inherited my practical side from Mother, along with her keen sense of observation and her drive. Interestingly, Mother's energy doubled as courage after we lost Father. She wept for a time, then one day got up, retired her mourning dresses, and engaged in rebuilding her life and finding a way of supporting her children. "No more black dresses, no more weeping," she said. Father, a teacher, had left us with limited resources and she had children to raise. People offered to help, but she refused and worked two jobs to support herself and the three of us.

I think that with my father gone, Mother came into her own, and spread her wings. Once she began earning a living, she was drunk with the sense of liberation it gave her. She had never worked outside the home and so had no experience or references to offer when she first applied for jobs. Eventually, when employers found out whose widow she was, they promptly hired her. My father's name and reputation was such that there were no questions asked. If she wanted it, she had a job, an expression of gratitude to Father from parents of students he had taught. Mother was a hard worker and no employer ever had reason to regret their generosity.

Father was a gentle yet demanding teacher, who brought out the best in his pupils, teaching by example and through stories, just as he taught me at home. Often, I sat opposite him on one of the matching chintz-covered chairs in the living room, comfortable and familiar, our special place for reading and story time. Because we spoke English, French, and Italian at home, we called this room "the lounge," "*le salon*," and "*il soggiorno*." My grandparents, who spoke Arabic, referred to it as "*El Salon*."

In summer, the first thing Father did was to throw open the shutters leading to the balcony, stretch, and exclaim about the beauty of the Mediterranean, whose every mood he enjoyed, he said. Once the room was aired out and cleaned, the shutters were closed. "It will keep the sun from bleaching the furniture," Mother said. We opened them again only in the late afternoon When these windows were wide open, the white sheers across them puffed up, catching the sea breezes. Nessim, Daniella, and I loved cocooning ourselves in them, twisting until we nearly yanked them off of their rods, or until we were reprimanded. Flies made themselves at home in our living room and we captured them and put them in a heavy pink glass vase, which my parents had received as a wedding gift. Nessim and Daniela covered this egg-shaped vase with a plate to keep their captives from escaping and did a body count at the end of each week, making notes like a pair of little scientists. I avoided this game as I did not like flies, even after Father showed me a picture of the gold flies worn by Ancient Egyptian generals as symbols of perseverance. "The fly buzzes," he said, "and we chase it away, but it keeps coming back. Little marauders they are, Maaya!" Still today, such memories come back so vividly they carry me to our apartment in Alexandria. I can smell the sea air and hear our shutters creak on their rusty hinges. I can hear Father reading and telling me stories, showing me a picture of Durga with her eight limbs. I remember almost word for word my father describing how she battled evil and vanquished the monster Mahishasura. I wanted to be like her.

I sat rapt as Father began in his gravelly smoker's voice:

"Once upon a time, a king was enticed by a beautiful buffalo and married her. The child born of their union was Mahishasura, half human and half beast. Mahishasura wanted to wage war against his enemies, the Devas, but he didn't want to die in battle. He made offerings to Brahma and begged him for the gift of immortality."

Here my father stopped and questioned me. This was part of our storytelling routine.

"Do you remember who Brahma is Maaya?" he asked.

"A Hindu God who created earth, Papa," I piped up, answer at the ready every time. "But tell me about Sasura, Papa, tell me about Sasura!" It was hard for me to pronounce the name, and so Mahishasura became Sasura and Durga became Dooga.

My father paused for effect. "Well, you know that Mahishasura wanted to never die. So, he asked Brahma to grant him one wish: to become immortal."

"Brahma granted him his wish, Papa?"

"Not quite, Maaya. But Brahma didn't want to deny him altogether, so he granted him a boon."

"What's a boon?"

"A gift, Maaya. Just like you are to Mama and me."

"What boon did Sasura get?"

"Brahma told Mahishasura that he would only die at the hands of a woman."

"Dooga?"

"It was, but Mahishasura didn't pay Brahma any mind when he heard this and just laughed so hard that tears rolled out of his eyes and down onto his belly."

"Why?"

"Because the monster did not believe that a woman could overpower him. But he was wrong." Here Father paused again, until I squirmed in my chair and asked, "And then? And then?"

"And then, my little Maaya, pride always comes before a fall."

My father had read the Bible cover to cover and many of his quotes came from Proverbs: "Pride goeth before destruction, and a haughty spirit before a fall." He loved sayings and proverbs as much as he loved stories, and he passed this love on to me. In a way, it was his special gift to his daughter, a gift that has kept on giving, a boon. To this day, I refer to sayings and stories to make sense of the world around me and because I love their poetry. They are seeds of wisdom that can be planted anytime, anywhere.

Proverbs and sayings used for effect in conversation is something I learned from listening to Egyptians talk. The use of known phrases or sayings provides common ground, a way to convey a message, a thought, and to include everyone in conversation. It is a tool for avoiding the superficial, the shallow when interacting, and also a way of not getting too personal. Proverbs go to the heart of a matter and serve, like mantras, to steady me. They can even console.

Mahishasura, my father explains when we get back to the story, is vain and proud. He does not believe for a moment that a female will be his nemesis. By the time Durga vanquishes the giant, he has already waged a bloody war against the Devas, his enemies, defeating them.

At this point in the story, I ask, "Did Sasura become a God after he defeated the Devas, Papa?"

"No, Maaya, and this is because he was not immortal, you see."

"But why?"

"The Devas were nearly decimated by Mahishasura. They had to do something. So they appealed to Brahma and made offerings to any god who would help them."

"Which gods, Papa?"

"The gods responsible for creating the world, Maaya."

"And then?"

"And then that's when Brahma and other gods created Durga to combat demons, and that is how Durga vanquished Mahishasura and saved the Devas."

At this point, my father tented his fingers, pointed them skyward, closed his eyes and whispered, "And now, my treasure, my sweet mulberry, it is time to say, "*Tuta, tuta, firghit al-hadduta*" (the story has been told).

He always ended stories with these nonsense words, learned from his Sephardic mother, whose mother tongue was Arabic. Always, I clamored for more and always my father responded, "Let's save some for another time."

This little scene I just played out is one of my happiest childhood memories.

My father's death affected me so profoundly, it nearly paralyzed me. Mother gave me time to grieve. Then one day, she walked into the living room in a light-blue dress and said to me as I wiped away tears, "Go wash your face, Maaya. Stand strong, and face your future. It is what Papa would have wanted you to do." She certainly was standing strong and facing her future, and I was expected to do the same. In a way, her stern (though not unkind) words stiffened my sagging backbone. Father continues to walk beside me, but my appetite for life has helped me overcome my grief at his departure.

I was in my last year of high school when Father died of a heart attack. His death was sudden and it was a shock. We had to adjust to his loss and also to our diminished resources. A schoolteacher's salary had not made us rich and our security was now compromised. I wanted to drop out of school and get a job, but Mother would not hear of it.

"You must graduate, Maaya," she insisted. "You are so smart, so close to finishing. I will talk to the Madame Santenac, the headmistress, to see if you can do some work after school." Soon, I had a job tutoring the children of a rich Alexandrian family and was able at the same time to study for my baccalaureate exams.

I failed the first time I sat for them, but the second time I passed, graduating from the Lycée Français where my father had taught.

I began to look for work after graduation. I went to see Mr. Mustacchi, proprietor of Cité du Livre and Father's friend. Loving books and people as I did, working in his bookstore would, I thought, be the perfect job for me. He hired me. I loved my job. I was in book heaven, learning to receive and catalogue new books. Mr. Mustacchi trained me to stock the shelves, and eventually to order books too. I loved getting acquainted with old and new titles, and with clients who loved to read. Part of my job was to discuss books with the distinguished clientele who came into Cité du Livre to browse, read, socialize, and buy books. I was in my element.

On Sunday mornings, we often had children and young readers at the bookstore. Mr. Mustacchi welcomed them, asked about their interests, encouraged them to keep reading, and was always ready to suggest books. He loved to say to them, "Reading brings us unknown friends," a quote from Honoré de Balzac, one of Mr. Mustacchi's favorite authors.

Many of the children who came to the bookstore were pupils from the European language schools scattered throughout the city, some secular like the English Girls'College and the Lycée Français in Chatby, some parochial like the prestigious Notre Dame de Sion. The bookshelves were stacked with books in many languages on many subjects, with a special section for children's books. We had comfortable chairs and small tables so people could relax while reading or meeting friends. Interesting people came in to browse, buy, order books, or just chat and look at some of the magazines Mr. Mustacchi offered. Our regulars included ambassadors; members of the Egyptian royal family; exiled foreign royalty like the king of Yugoslavia, the queen of Bulgaria, and the heir to the Italian throne and his wife; prominent Egyptians, many of whom were Francophiles and Anglophiles, and prominent Jews like the Menasces and the Aghions, to name a few. The Turkish ambassador to Egypt came in every afternoon, bringing with him cakes. We became friends, had tea together, and talked about books. It was a very pleasant atmosphere.

Cité du Livre was located at 2 Rue Fuad next to the Café Patisserie Baudrot, where we bought pastries and petits fours. The street itself was a symbol of Alexandria's grand history, with elegant villas and antique shops—a historic street, where the novelist Lawrence Durrell and the poet Constantine Cavafy once lived. It was named after King Fuad of Egypt, father of King Faruq, last king of Egypt, who was ousted after the bloodless revolution of 1952. As King Fuad died shortly before I was born, I came into the world along with this new (and last) reigning monarch of Egypt, Faruq, who left Egypt forever with his family on board his yacht, the *Mahroosa*, and died in exile.

I have always had a person of special significance, someone of special importance in my life. The first such person was, of course, my father. The next was my maternal grandmother, who came to live with us after my father died. Then, when I was fifteen, there was Ezra, who introduced me to Zionism and became my life partner.

You asked me what drew me to the Zionist movement? I will tell you. I was drawn to the Zionist movement because I wanted to meet boys and girls like me, and I stayed in the movement because of Ezra. Here's the story.

Ezra had been sent by the Cairo headquarters of the Zionist movement to teach us ideology and activism. "You Alexandrians are a superficial bunch," they said. "You are unfocused and shallow, but we will soon change you." The organization intended to send someone to pull us together, to draw us into the movement and out of what they called "your complacency." For months, the rumor was that a certain Ezra was coming to fulfill this mission. So, we kept an eye out for the said Ezra, and we waited and waited and waited. No Ezra, no Ezra, no Ezra came. However, one day, almost a year after he was promised, here he was. Our first meeting was comedic. I'll never forget the scene.

Ezra arrived in Alexandria and our group called a meeting, which I came to attend. I was expecting nothing more than a lighthearted get-together with a little ideology mixed in. I walked into the apartment where these meetings were held. There indeed was Ezra, standing on a ladder, nailing up a huge black-and-white poster of the Dome of the Rock to one wall. He looked so comical that I giggled, as did my friends. Others joined our giggle fest and wanted to know why we were so amused. We said, "This little guy, this funny-looking fellow is the Ezra Cairo was so excited about? Really?" Ezra looked like a boy, not a mature man. He was short, slight, with a large head, short arms and legs, a round face, and round hazel eyes. His nose and mouth could have been modeled after those of a clown. In short, he looked like a cartoon character, this elusive Ezra who had been sent to make something of our ragtag troupe, to motivate and organize us. Looking up at him, my buddy Anya declared, "This is the emissary who is going to whip us into shape? My, my, my, what are they thinking in Cairo?" I laughed out loud, Ezra looked around, registered our amusement, and came down off his ladder. He must have been used to this reaction, because instead of frowning, he introduced himself with a smile. And that was when I fell in love. Let me tell you, what Ezra lacked in looks, he made up for in charm and, I eventually found out, in intelligence. There was something about him, a *je ne sais quoi*, which instantly piqued your curiosity in a nice way. It is hard to describe. What is it about certain people that just captures your attention, and sometimes more than your attention? As I got to know Ezra better and better, I experienced his charisma and also admired his dedication to the cause of a homeland for the Jews. He had purpose and he projected confidence in his purpose. Can you tell I'm still in love with Ezra?

My father was surprised when I joined the Zionist movement, because he himself was a freethinker and had raised us with mostly secular ideals. Of course, he went along with the traditions my mother set down, such as the celebration of high holidays and Shabbat meals. On Fridays she made sofrito: braised chicken with lemon, cardamom, and turmeric. She always made extra, which we enjoyed eating cold the next day. She had learned to cook this dish from her observant Syrian mother, whose traditional values impressed themselves on our family, especially when she moved in with us after Father died.

While my father never denied his Jewish roots, he took a more intellectual approach to Judaism than my mother and her family did. This might be explained in part by events in his childhood. His mother was a Christian and his father a Jew. Both parents were teachers who had come to Egypt seeking opportunities and for health reasons. His mother had pulmonary problems. Father said, "She had fragile lungs." The mild, dry climate of Egypt helped her. Not for long, though, as both she and my grandfather died in an automobile accident shortly after settling in Egypt. This is when he, his sister, and his brother were taken in by their mother's family and sent to a boarding school, where they learned English and French, and where the religious classes were Christian teachings. I am saying that I think he was influenced by the Christian milieu of his mother's family. Clearly neither Christianity nor Judaism satisfied him completely, as he sought other spiritual traditions—Buddhism and Hinduism.

When my father fell in love with my mother, he knew he would be marrying into a devout Sephardic family who kept a kosher household. He knew they observed the rites and rituals of Judaism. He went along, but was never committed. My parents' marriage was not what you would call ideal, but somehow they survived their differences. My mother's family had objected, but could not prevail upon their daughter to give up this man she had fallen head over heels in love with. "I will marry him with or without your blessings," she is said to have threatened. Her parents acquiesced, preferring to let her go and not to lose her to bad blood. Interestingly, my maternal grandmother, a sweet-natured, intelligent woman, eventually grew very fond of Father and he of her. He was considerate of her feelings too, and when she came to visit, he made sure we did not have certain foods in the house, like pork. My mother kept a set of tableware aside for her, dedicated it to her use only, and cooked according to traditions. She followed the Halacha, the Jewish law, when my grandmother came to live with us, bringing with her traditions and teachings that fascinated me.

My grandmother Sarah was diminutive and very fair, her skin crinkled when she smiled, with one gold tooth showing. I remember best her exceptionally small hands and feet, her long white hair wrapped in a Syrian-style *mandeel*, a kerchief with a dainty lace border. When she visited us, she brought treats, particularly M&M's, a handful in each tiny packet she made of bits of fabric left over from sewing our clothes. These she tucked in between the blankets in the linen closet, which is why they always smelled and tasted of mothballs. Whenever I eat them today, my mind plays tricks on me and I get a whiff of mothballs along with the taste of chocolate.

My grandmother's father was a rabbi and, as Sarah was an only child, he raised her like a son, teaching her Hebrew and reading to her from the Torah. She spoke Arabic, read some Hebrew, and was devout. She was unusual in that she did not impose teachings or traditions on us children. Rather, she taught by example, using Arabic sayings and proverbs. Father collected them in a pocket-sized notepad he called 'Sarah's sayings.' When I stumbled on it after Father died, I wept and wept and wept. My grandmother stroked me and said, "What soap is for the body, tears are for the soul, Maaya. Cry, child. Cry until the tears have washed this sadness from your heart." When my father had been gone a year, she said, "One should not grieve too much for the dead. Those who grieve too much and too long are really grieving for someone other than their loved one, maybe for themselves." This reflection, I learned, came straight from the *Shulchan Aruch*, a sixteenth-century book that detailed Sephardic laws and customs.

My grandmother taught me a great deal of what I had missed under my parents' tutelage, gently introducing me to the Halacha, the collective body of Jewish religious laws derived from the Torah. Just as I had been fascinated by the stories from mythology told me by my father, I became fascinated with Judaism and soon began to study. When Ezra came along, I was receptive to everything Jewish, including the ideal of a Jewish homeland.

My grandmother spoke Arabic, French, Italian, and Spanish. She had worked as a lady's companion to the dowager of a rich Jewish family from Italy living in Egypt. She was a paid companion, what we called "*une dame de compagnie*." She spoke Italian fluently and taught it to my mother, and often that was the language they spoke at home. She was dignified and generous, loved by all who knew her.

For a time, my grandmother's family had lived in Palestine, in Safed, where there has always been a Jewish community. She was there until she turned sixteen. When she met a Jewish family from Egypt, she went to work for them. This family was religious and kept a kosher household, and so did Sarah. She was inspired by this family's refined lifestyle and piety, and when she married and had children, she taught them what she had learned in that time.

My grandmother had two daughters and two sons, and all but my mother left to study in Europe before World War II. One died in a Nazi concentration camp and one returned to live in Paris, but had become blind due to the hardships he experienced in the camps. Mother remained safely in Egypt, until such a time as we were forced to leave. She could never get used to being away from Egypt. In Israel, where our exodus had first taken us, she never felt at home.

I left Egypt in 1949 to join Ezra in Paris, and eventually we were married and lived in France for several years before moving to Israel and eventually to the United States. I was caught up in Ezra's idealism, becoming aware of what he referred to as "the Jewish problem." It had never occurred to me that as a Jew I would encounter any sort of difficulty assimilating into French society, especially as I spoke French fluently. Nor did I ever question feeling at home in Egypt, but not really being at home in Egypt. It is hard to explain, but I can say this: We lived in Egypt and thought we would die in Egypt, yet we never really assimilated. Egyptians too saw us as foreigners and perhaps this is why many of us felt drawn to a Jewish homeland, a place that would help end our wandering, would truly be ours, a haven for body and soul.

Ezra helped me to understand the need for a homeland for the Jews. His was a way of thinking so different from my father's, whose word had been gospel to me such that it took my falling in love with Ezra to stray from his mentorship. Father saw no reason whatever to go to Palestine or to live in a Jewish state. He repeated, "*Il n'y a aucune raison de vivre exclusivement avec les Juifs*" (There is no reason whatsoever to live exclusively among Jews). Ezra, on the other hand, would counter this with quotes like the one he shared with me from Yigal Allon, a Jewish politician he admired: "Zionism is the redemption of an ancient nation from a tragic lot . . . " Or he would recite from Ilya Ehrenburg: "You trace your roots to Abraham, Jewish nation, O nation once powerful and grand . . . " Ezra added, "And so it shall be once more." He had charisma and I was swept along in the wake of his enthusiasm and dedication.

When I became interested in political movements and ideologies, my father readily discussed them with me, but he found it difficult to understand why I was drawn to Zionism. Of course, it was initially because I was smitten with Ezra, as I said, and his purpose-driven life. Ezra belonged to a group of youths who were engaged in social activism, and for whom world issues were important. The closer I got to Ezra, the more I began to feel moved by the idea of a Jewish homeland, the creation of a State of Israel. At the age of nineteen one is easily drawn to new ideas, new possibilities. I was no exception. I was moved to tears one day when Ezra quoted Paula Buber, writer and wife of famous German philosopher Martin Buber: "You ancient people, you wonderful people, how I love you people of sorrow!" In Egypt, I had not thought of us as a people of sorrow, but Ezra opened my eyes to our history and convinced me of the need for a nation we could call our own. At the time, I was not thinking of what would become of the Palestinians who laid claim to the same land.

The Agence Juive in Paris was aware of Ezra's Zionist activities in Egypt, which is why they hired him. All the while, he explained that our time in France was not more than an interlude. His goal was to get to Israel. He was five years older than me and very persuasive. Ezra made up in charisma what he lacked in looks. He identified with Léon Blum, who was three times prime minister of France and who declared, "I am a Jew . . . that is a fact . . . I belong to a Jewish race, that race I have never denied and I have only feelings of gratitude and pride toward it."

We were in love, Ezra and I. When I fell for him, I also fell under the spell of the Zionist movement and all of the eloquent people who spoke in favor of it and labored to make the dream of a Jewish homeland a reality. Having common ideals strengthened our love and our commitment.

The Paris years were stimulating and memorable. I blossomed and basked in the atmosphere of culture. Paris was the essence of culture. I could not take it all in, obviously, but drank from its fountain as much as I could. I loved the museums, theaters, concerts, streets, food . . . everything. Really, I couldn't get enough of it. I was starved for something more than what Alexandria had offered me. You know, despite the mystery surrounding Alexandria, it was really very small and confining by comparison. Of course, there were significant pockets of intellectual and artistic activity, there were sophisticated groups of people, but the public side of culture was limited. In Paris, the breadth of culture was breathtaking.

Ezra and I lived in a clean, modest pension. We ate out all the time. I had no household responsibilities to speak of and enjoyed the freedom. I had plenty of time to explore Paris and its environs and take in as much culture as I wished. We lived on Ezra's salary, which was enough to pay for these modest lodgings and reasonably priced (but excellent) meals at neighborhood restaurants. When Ezra was not working, we explored and discovered Paris together and Paris remained a highlight of our married life, a destination on a number of our anniversaries.

During our early years together, Ezra and I were high on our newfound freedom, but we were also very young and opinionated, and fought all the time. It was really about insignificant things, things hardly worth fighting over. Yet our marriage held. I think it was because we cared so much about each other and ultimately enjoyed sharing life's journey together more than apart. Sometimes today we laugh about the tiffs and the flying feathers. "How did you manage?" people who had seen us fight over the years asked. I said, "Oh, it all adds spice to our marriage!"

Ezra worked and was focused on his mission, while I had a lot of time on my hands as he did not want me to work. So, when I was not out exploring Paris, I sat at a café or tucked into our small room and began to write about my life in Egypt. The stories I am recounting here are based on my journals, which are filled with details so vivid they are etched in my memory.

Growing up, I had a great sense of independence because Mother was not a worrier. We children did pretty much what we wanted and Alexandria was safe, so there was no danger in going out alone or in groups. Every summer, the family rented what we called 'huts' directly on the beach at Abukir, about an hour or so from Alexandria. The atmosphere was relaxed. The entire three months we spent there we lived in our swimsuits and pajamas. As soon as school was out, we were ready to go. Luckily, because Father was a schoolteacher, we had the same holiday schedules. The beaches of Abukir were clean, uncrowded, and quiet, the atmosphere and the pace of life rejuvenating. We played, read, slept, loafed, napped anytime we felt like it, and ate at local casinos (fish restaurants) whenever no one was in the mood to cook. We got together with people who vacationed there regularly, or with newfound friends to play cards in the evening or have drinks and meze, which Father called '*amuse-gueule*,' palate teasers—appetizers, really. We kids went exploring, looked for Napoleon's fort, swam, sunned, played ball on the beach, or waited for the fishing boats to return with their catch of the day, often sardines. We deep-fried them, eating them like chips. The first few days, we invariably stayed too long outdoors and ended up with sunburns, but then our skin became seasoned, or perhaps we grew more careful. Happy times!

The beaches of Alexandria were beautiful too. We enjoyed the huge waves at Chatby, the two beautiful bays at Sporting, the white sands of Stanley and Sidi Bishr. There was always something to do. I could not remember a time when we were ever bored. Alexandria was a walking city and there was also a good system of tramways, which we used to go to Stanley, because it was too far to walk. I walked so much that by the time I was fifteen, I had developed sturdy calf muscles worthy of an athlete.

Mother never asked us to get home at any particular time, but by the time I became a teenager Father kept an eye on me and insisted I be home at a certain time in the evening. I lost him the year I turned sixteen and Mother was not too worried about my safety. However, I can tell you that girls in Egypt were very protected once they reached puberty. Parents were afraid that daughters might lose their virginity, dishonor their families, and ruin their lives.

One year a friend fell in love and in a moment of folly succumbed to her lover's charms. Her ensuing pregnancy was a cause of terrible shame to her family, who sent her away for a year and arranged for the child to be adopted by an older, married sister.

We always socialized in groups and this was a sort of safeguard against temptations and their consequences. Schoolteachers too were vigilant, as strict with the boys as with the girls. Friendships, as I recall, were a question of personal affinity. I had Armenian, Greek, and Egyptian friends through all of my years at school, but when it came to marrying, people usually stuck to their own groups. There were exceptions, of course. My friends Cecile and Dora married Muslim men. Another, nicknamed Foufa, fell in love with a Copt and was shipped out of the country to "cool off," her parents said. A fourth, Adiva, had somehow caught the eye of the young and lecherous King Faruq, who invited her to tea at the palace. She was seventeen. Her parents found the royal interest in their daughter terrifying and wrote to thank him saying, "We are not worthy of such an honor, Your Majesty," and promptly sent her to live with family in Italy for an entire year.

When I think of Egypt, I think of food. I think of the afternoons spent with my friends, how we went to each other's houses, shared snacks like sandwiches made with *dukka*, a mixture of herbs and sesame seeds. When I speak to friends, they too tell me that they associate Egypt with food and smells. Remembering the garlands of jasmine perfuming the air in summer, we laugh at how peddlers came up to open car windows, reached in without asking, and hung two or three strands on rearview mirrors. Few drivers refused to pay them. The perfume was intoxicating. We savored food at home too, or sitting in seaside cafés. We enjoyed street foods like grilled corn on the cob along the corniche in Alexandria in summer. There were pastries dripping with syrup, thin sesame wafers, which vendors carried in a glass case balanced on one shoulder or on their heads to sell on the beaches. And, of course, there was that Egyptian favorite, *libb* (toasted pumpkin or watermelon seeds, dusted with salt), twisted into newspaper or butcher-paper cornets, their shells littering the streets in the wake of strollers or the floors of movie theaters, where they were consumed like popcorn. The smell and sounds of the sea permeated everything.

There are so many odd little memories that pop up unexpectedly: The shoe shop Mother took us to and the sturdy white sandals she bought for summer wear, the lace-up shoes for school. The vendor wrapped a sock around our knuckles to approximate the size shoe we needed. Could this be why my shoes did not fit half the time? So many images, so many memories! What more can I say? Egypt stays with you.

7
Pilar

Meeting Pilar

Pilar was striking. Tall, slender, green-eyed, she radiated serenity. She had an aquiline nose and a tiny mouth, glossy with pink lipstick. Her fair skin crinkled in a friendly way when she smiled, and her hands were equally expressive. Using them to gesture as she spoke, she tried out a number of Arabic phrases on me as soon as I arrived. She wore a gold wedding band and an emerald ring set with diamonds on her left hand. The emerald, she said, was her birthstone and had been a gift from her late husband. As I got to know her, I saw that she favored pastel colors, pantsuits, flat Belgian shoes, and pearls. Her honey-colored bouffant hairdo was just as her daughter, Cecile, remembered it all her life.

I met Cecile while auditing a class on Middle Eastern literature at Columbia University. We became friends and it was she who introduced me to Pilar, now a widow, assuring me that her mother, once she got to know me, would agree to my recording her story. "She loves to talk about her memories of Egypt," Cecile said.

When I called on Pilar, at her small apartment on the East River, I noted the chintz curtains drawn, probably to preserve the furniture and the richly colored Persian rug set on top of white wall-to-wall carpeting. The apartment was fragrant with the scent of cinnamon, which Pilar soon explained: "I made *erfa* (sweet cinnamon tea) for us," she said. She served it with chopped nuts and milk, "*zayy fi Masr* (just like in Egypt)," she said with a smile, offering me a slice of her homemade pound cake.

After a number of visits, she agreed to allow me to turn on my tape recorder and proceeded to remember "my Egypt." When first she interjected her story with Arabic words, she got a twinkle in her eye and stopped to say, "*shufi, ana ma-nsitshi*" (See, I have not forgotten). Indeed, she had not. Here is her story.

Pilar tells her story

My mother's name was Mazal and my father's name was Salama. I think our family name, Toledano, indicates that our ancestors came from Spain, maybe Toledo. They migrated to Syria in the fifteenth century to escape persecution.

My mother was only fourteen when she married my father. He first saw her walking by in front of his father's shop in their hometown of Aleppo. Instantly, he was smitten. Her sweetness and her poise were her chief assets, and he loved her for them. He told his parents and they went to her parents to ask for her hand. As my father was a steady young man with a good reputation, her family soon agreed and prepared her dowry. Though my father saw my mother, she did not meet him until close to the time of their wedding. He was ten years older—quiet, kindhearted, and devoted to her all of their lives. It was a good match.

A year after my parents married they had their first son, Abraham, followed by my second brother, Yosef, and another after him, Daniel, and finally Daoud. He would be their last, or so they thought. Daoud was a babe in arms when my parents Mazal and Salama left Syria to seek their fortune in Egypt. And then, lo and behold, five years later, they had me and named me Pilar after a neighbor in Cairo who became like a sister to my mother. We children grew up together in harmony. My brothers were very protective of me.

My father was from a middle-class family with middle-class means. When business started to falter in Syria, he decided to move to Egypt, where my mother had family in Cairo. They helped Father get started in business.

My parents sent Abraham and Yosef to the Jesuit schools, but when it came time to send Daoud and Daniel, funds were lacking. They decided to keep one home and scrape together enough to send the brighter of the two to get an education. The Jesuit fathers found a way to keep them both as scholarship students, however.

My parents did not feel that a girl needed an education, and so I was only sent for a short time to learn to read, write, and count. I attended a school run by Catholic sisters in Sakakini. I was an intelligent child and felt I had been deprived of something I wanted very much—an education.

I made up for it throughout my life by reading and educating myself. Of course, I was expected to help my mother at home, and learned to cook and sew at her side. She taught me how to set a table for the holidays and generally all I needed to know to be a capable housewife. On the third Wednesday of the month, my mother invited a few of her friends to our house for tea. She took out the silver tray, forks, knives, spoons, and a set of tea glasses in silver sleeves. In the Syrian manner, jams were served with tea, each guest taking a spoonful then setting it in a glass of water on the tray. I was expected to help and be a dutiful daughter, and I tried to be, though I never liked these women's gatherings. Too much chatter, too much gossip!

My father was kind, but he also had a temper. My mother, on the other hand, was pure honey, always loving, always patient, always attentive. I wondered if my father's short temper might have been the result of not being as successful in business as he had hoped. One thing I know is that the boys had to go to work elsewhere, not with him in his shop. My brother Abraham worked at Sednaoui, a famous Cairo department store. He went out every night and was a womanizer, which my father did not like. One night in particular stands out. My brother arrived home late one night in a taxi. He was drunk, shouting and making a racket because the taxi driver wanted payment and my brother had lost his money. Abraham caused my father a lot of pain as the years went on. He drank and then went on to smoke hashish and to pilfer money from all of us. I had a little pouch with my savings, which I kept in a drawer under a few pictures and handkerchiefs. He helped himself even to my money. He was very, very sweet and always coddled and kissed me, his baby sister, but this did not keep him from stealing the little bit I had saved from the embroidery work that I did on commission.

Yosef, on the other hand, was the responsible one. He did so well in school that he was able to get what the government called a 'mission' to go abroad, having first studied at Cairo University. At first he attended day classes, then night classes, going to work in the day and also helping Father at the store. Eventually, he was sent to England, where he studied textile engineering and became successful. Upon his return to Egypt, he worked as an engineer for the mills in the town of Kafr al-Dawwar. They produced beautiful wool cloth for suits. Yosef soon moved to France, where he married a Frenchwoman and raised a family of three boys and a girl. He lived and died in Lyon.

Daoud worked in a large establishment in the Hamzawi district of Cairo. He made money right away. One day, however, on his way home, he was struck by a tram and died. His loss was very hard on our family. Daniel tried to compensate by working and spending time at home, but he also liked to go out with his friends. Once, when I was fifteen, he brought home a friend and introduced us, saying, "He is a good boy. You can go out with us if you wish." My parents were outraged. I never did go out with this boy.

One day, Abraham said, "Yosef is now living abroad and I want to do the same." My father said, "Where are you going to go, tell me that." My brother said, "I don't know yet." But I think he knew. One day he packed his bags, kissed each of us goodbye, and left. We were all at the dining-room table and my father neither got up, nor accompanied him to the train station. He called him a bad seed, an ungrateful wretch. It was very hard parting on such bad terms. Abraham went to Panama, counting on Yosef, it seems, to send him money. Meanwhile, Daniel remained at home, diligent and hardworking. He wanted to fill the void left by his brothers. Strangely, Father did not appreciate his qualities as much as he should have. He took Daniel for granted.

One day we heard news of Abraham. He was going somewhere by boat and had met a man on board who befriended him. They chatted and the conversation turned to marriageable women. The man showed Abraham a picture of his married sister standing with another girl who was her friend. Abraham asked the man: "May I write to your sister's friend?" The man gave him an address in Italy. He wrote and they corresponded for a time, exchanging information about their families and so on. This woman's name was Aldina. She told her brother of her pen pal and gave him the address Abraham had given her for the family in Egypt. The brother then wrote to us, saying, "My sister has been corresponding with Abraham and would like to marry him." My father charged my brother Daniel with responding. And Daniel wrote back: "I cannot be responsible for this marriage. My brother has no money. I don't know what he does in life and I cannot guarantee him." Abraham was handsome and charming, you see, and women fell for him. So, as we used to say, "*men hena leh hena*" (from here to there and back again). Aldina decided to take a chance on him. They met and married. Abraham managed to make a living of some sort, but nothing too special. Aldina's family was in textiles in Italy and they must have helped to support them. She was not a beauty and she was almost forty when she married my brother. Perhaps that is why the family accepted him. We had a saying, "*dall ragel walla dall heita*" (A woman is better having the shadow of any man than the shadow of a wall). Aldina was under Abraham's spell and put up with him even though he never stopped chasing skirts, as they say, and had countless mistresses. Meanwhile, I was growing up. A friend who had just married a man from a rich Jewish family invited me for tea one day and said, "My husband has a cousin who is steady and good who would like to meet you." So I did, but I was already in love with a young man, a friend of Daniel's whom I had met when I was fourteen years old. He was not from a rich family. In fact, his family were very modest people, but I never loved anyone else. His name was Ezra Naphtali, and he eventually became my husband.

My parents said, "You are young and pretty and there are a lot of rich boys who would be glad to marry you. What kind of prospects does this Ezra have?"

Another problem for both the Naphtalis and the Toledanos was that Ezra's family were Ashkenazi and we were Sephardi Jews. Neither family was in favor of this marriage. Their objections were to no avail. Ezra and I loved each other and were determined to marry. I was seventeen and Ezra was nineteen when we did, even though our parents forbade us from seeing each other. Ezra showed no interest in anyone but me, and I wanted only Ezra.

Ezra's family said, "Why go after this Sephardic girl when you can have your cousin so-and-so and a dowry of 2,000 Egyptian pounds? Or the daughter of so-and-so with a dowry of 3,000 Egyptian pounds?" An uncle declared, "I will give you my daughter and an apartment of your own plus a yearly stipend." Ezra would have none of it and I would have no other. We must have been a handful to our families!

Ezra was nothing special, really, but he was honest and kind, calm and steady, tender, nice looking, neat in his appearance, and clean. This meant something to me. I knew the value of these qualities, even though I was so young. Maybe seeing how Abraham was with women was an early lesson of what to avoid. I had known Ezra two years and had never heard him utter a harsh word to anyone. True, he worked in a pharmacy—a modest job and income—but it was Ezra I grew to like and to love, and it was Ezra I wanted. He felt the same way about me. Keep in mind that in those days marriage was a negotiation. Often, marriage within families was a way to tighten the tribal knot and keep resources from going out of the family. Ezra told our families that if they stood in our way we would never marry.

Ezra did not care that I did not have a dowry and I cared only that he was honest and kind, however modest his income was.

"How can you marry her with not a cent to her name?" people asked. Ezra responded, "Her smile is her dowry and her laughter is the wealth that brightens my heart."

I said, "It's Ezra or no one at all."

My parents finally relented and his family accepted me, albeit reluctantly, as they wanted an Ashkenazi girl. Well, both families would have preferred one of their own kind. Ezra and I married and lived happily ever after. I will fill you in on a few of the details that led up to our wedding.

My brother Daniel came to my father one day and said, "Why are you working so hard to keep Pilar and Ezra from marrying? He is from an honest family. It's true he's not rich, but he is honest and hardworking, and she wants him. So what if he's not rich? He'll make his way and Pilar wants them to make their way together. Do you want her to be an old maid?" It was really Daniel who persuaded my father to let me have my way. My father finally said to me, "You want Ezra? Tell him to come to our house for dinner tonight." Ezra came. It was his first 'official' visit to me at our house, as before then we had met in secret, Ezra sending a signal through my brother. We used to meet in front of the Chemla department store downtown. We pretended to be window-shopping as we stood next to each other and talked. We talked and talked and talked, and every now and again stole a little kiss. That's all. My pretext for going to Chemla was that I needed samples of fabric. I accumulated quite a collection of samples, but was always home by five in the afternoon, never later. When my father returned from his shop at six, I was on the sofa, reading or fingering my samples in full view of the family, getting opinions on what I should get for my next dress or nightgown. Everyone had an opinion and it was in this way that I diverted their attention from why I was really going to Chemla. Sewing was my bridge to Ezra.

The night Ezra was expected for dinner, my parents made one last stab at what they called "bringing me to my senses." They said, "Pilar, do you really want to live in poverty? This is where you are headed." Silence was my response. When Ezra arrived, my heart melted. I knew he was the one. After dinner, he and I sat on the balcony of my parents' apartment overlooking Midan Tawfiqiya. Mother sat on the sofa in the living room with the doors open, keeping an eye on us.

Ezra and I felt no pleasure in being together with so many restrictions. We wanted to get married. He had a motorcycle with a sidecar, which he and my brother Daniel owned together. After we were engaged, he used to take me for rides after work. Meanwhile, I prepared a modest trousseau and, with the help of a seamstress who came to the house, I made a few dresses, including my wedding dress.

I should tell you that it was about six months after that first dinner that Ezra and I looked at each other in earnest and said, "We are going to get married." And so we went to the rabbinate. Those who were present in Egypt from Ezra's family and from mine attended. There were some twenty people. That's all.

After the wedding my parents went home but Ezra's brothers said, "We must celebrate the marriage of Ezra and Pilar." They opened a bottle of champagne, or maybe it was beer—I can't remember, as I don't drink—and that same evening we took the train to Alexandria and began our week-long honeymoon. We spent our wedding night at a nice little hotel by the sea. Ezra was to meet a client one day that same week to get paid some money that was owed him. The man came and we had a few extra pounds to spend on our honeymoon.

Marriage is not about money. When you get married, it has to do with you and with me, although families, of course, get involved, sometimes for the good and other times in a destructive way. Ezra and I were the youngest son and the youngest daughter of our families. My parents gave us their blessing on one condition: We would all move to a bigger apartment and live together.

Ezra and I lived with my parents for almost two years. What was their motivation, you ask? Perhaps they wanted to be sure their only daughter would be safe, or maybe they could not stand to part with me. Perhaps it was a financial consideration as they would, given Ezra's salary, have had to help us if we had been renting an apartment on our own. After I became pregnant, they did make their peace with my decision to marry Ezra but it took them a while to accept that we wanted to live on our own once our baby was born.

The year Cecile was born, Daniel married a girl from a well-to-do family. This was a consolation to my parents. Although they had outwardly accepted Ezra, it was never clear if they did in their hearts. Life with my parents became more and more difficult, and within a few months of my giving birth at home, my father began to grumble: "She cries all night and keeps me awake," or, "You put her on the sofa and look, it's all wet," and so on. It was definitely time to go.

When our baby turned one, we found an apartment in the Carlo Grassi Building, on what became known as Sherif Pasha Street. It had four large rooms, a large foyer, and a big kitchen. The rent was six Egyptian pounds a month. We took it, deciding we would use part of it as an office for Ezra. And that's just what we did. Our first dining-room table was a board set on sawhorses, which I covered with piece of off-white linen, a remnant from Sednaoui, a fabric store. I embroidered an array of flowers and bows in the center and this tablecloth served us for years. Gradually, we feathered our nest as Ezra went into the construction business and made good. Ezra was ingenious and hardworking, and little by little our situation improved. We were happy—happy together, happy with our little girl.

The hardest times for me were when Ezra had to travel. He went to villages all over Egypt and his jobs were timed by the rise and fall of the Nile. He could not build when it flooded. I wanted to learn about these 'moods' of the Nile, as I liked to call them when discussing Ezra's building ventures. One day, I heard of a lecture to be given at the French Archeological Institute and persuaded Ezra to take me there to hear it. We left Cecile with my parents and went out for a rare evening on our own. The lecturer caught my attention when he said that the Ancient Egyptians believed flooding was the result of the goddess Isis's tears flowing as she grieved for her dead husband. In fact, it is the result of monsoons in the Ethiopian highlands dumping rain into the Nile, starting in spring and continuing through most of the summer. In August, the humidity rose as a result and we had to be careful with heat rash. I kept medicated talcum powder on hand for Cecile. It relieved the itching. If it were not for the Nile, Egypt would have been a desert, of course. Along with the discomforts of summer, there was a sense of exhilaration that came with the flooding. Strange! I can still feel it all these years later. They say "the body remembers," and if my experience is an indication of this, I'd say it is true.

Before Ezra went into business he worked at the Pharmacie Delmar, downtown. As I said, he was ingenious. When he told me about one of his schemes we laughed goodheartedly about it. To supplement his income, Ezra bought old magazines on the cheap. They were a little risqué. He cut out pictures of women, put them on cardboard with a ribbon around them for a frame, and sold them under the counter. He always found ways of making money.

Ezra and my brother Daniel were good friends. They spent a lot of time together. It was Daniel who introduced Ezra to the writings of Karl Marx and talked to him about unionizing the pharmacy workers. When he tried, Ezra was fired, but a friend of his father's intervened on his behalf, begging the owner to consider this nothing more than youthful folly. The owner agreed, but docked Ezra's pay two pounds. All of this was before we married.

After we married, he went to work in a village, supervising workers in plaster, and slowly built up his business from there. Little by little, we furnished our apartment nicely and improved our lot. As he became more experienced, Ezra joined a cousin in his construction business, and their enterprises grew. He worked for the private sector and also took on government contracts, working with Greek, Yugoslav, and Egyptian engineers. He knew French and we spoke French at home, and sometimes he did work for French companies too. He eventually had three hundred Egyptians working under him, before he and his cousin went their separate ways.

In the 1930s, when land was cheap, Ezra bought land in Zamalek and talked to me about building there. I went to my father and asked if he wished to be in on this venture. My father by then had mellowed. He said, "*Allah yekhalleek, ya Ezra*" (May God protect you, Ezra). He admitted that Ezra was a good man, honest and respectful of our traditions. Spending holidays with our families, he never failed to be attentive to my parents, even in the early days when they did not treat him so well. He was one of ten children and the last child of the family, and had to fend for himself. When it came time to be 'bar-mitzvahed,' his parents just said to him, "Go to the temple, Ezra." So, Ezra went to the temple alone and returned home. There was no fuss made over him. He was a good man, a self-made man.

Ezra's parents were devout and kept a kosher home, and both our parents celebrated the holidays. When they came to our house, I respected the traditions. On the first two nights of Rosh Hoshana, we went to my parents first, then to Ezra's. It was always very cheerful at the Naphtali family's table. Ezra's parents and his brothers got along well and the wives got along well and everyone was full of good humor. Some of the wives were Ladino and spoke Spanish. Often we sang and the prayers lasted for hours.

Eventually, when Ezra finished the construction of the Zamalek property, we rented all of the apartments and had good income from them. We would have liked to live there, but thought better of living in a building where we had renters. So we stayed where we were, although Ezra no longer had his office in our apartment. We gradually became financially secure and traveled more. Later, we moved to a bigger apartment in midtown Cairo and furnished it elegantly from top to bottom. We had an English-style dining room, a Louis XVI salon, and all the comforts I could want.

I like to improve myself and I learned a lot through reading. I have also always enjoyed books on interior decorating and the home arts. My first one, a gift from Ezra, was bought secondhand from the bookstalls of Azbakiya. I enjoyed looking at the pictures, though I did not read it, as it was in German. It was copiously illustrated with black-and-white photos and was entitled *Shone Wohnung* (Pretty Home). Later, after we left Egypt and got settled in New York, I took classes in the decorative arts. It was a new world opening up to me, a world unlike the one I grew up in.

When I was a little girl, I never went on vacations. The Toledanos were very modest people. Once Ezra's prospects improved and we began to feel secure, we took vacations. We went to Alexandria, rented an apartment, and brought with us a little maid to help me with Cecile and with cooking. Actually, the first time, we stayed at a pension, then at a hotel, then rented an apartment. Eventually, we began to travel to Europe.

We had made a good life for ourselves in Egypt, but by the 1950s the Jews were no longer welcome. We soon left, taking only the clothes on our backs, a small suitcase each, and $200. We started over in New York, and as you can see the rest is history. We had struggles and made adjustments, but once again Ezra made a way for us as he had in Egypt. Our daughter is now happily married and has five children. When Ezra died, she found me a small apartment near her and helped me to move. I have found consolation in spending time with Cecile and her family and in doing volunteer work.

Life goes on.

8
Ariadne

Meeting Ariadne

Meeting Ariadne at a dinner party in New York hosted by mutual friends provided me with a companion to pal around with. We took to each other, despite some distinctly different political views. We agreed to disagree and kept our conversations on neutral ground. We lived a few blocks apart, which made it easy for us to become walking companions.

I had moved uptown to 1270 Fifth Avenue, on the edge of Spanish Harlem. She lived a few blocks down, in the upscale Nineties. We were both single and could easily meet at a moment's notice, which we often did in Central Park. We especially enjoyed the changing seasons at the Conservatory Gardens, located midway between us. We also visited museums and attended film festivals. Once we attended the film screening of *Exodus* on a very cold night in January 1997, walking to the Jewish Museum bundled up like Eskimos. It was not Otto Preminger's *Exodus*, but a documentary film. Ariadne and I discussed this movement, which catapulted the United Nations into making a resolution to partition Palestine, creating a home for the Jewish people. The film, narrated by Morley Safer, left an impression on us both for different reasons. We parted in a thoughtful mood that evening, walking in silence.

Ariadne was tall and generously built, though not fat or heavy for her almost six feet. She had a peaches-and-cream complexion, a narrow, heart-shaped face, a 'distinguished' nose, and full lips she painted bright red. She had a full head of long hair dyed jet black, which she wore in a braid or an upsweep. Her eyes, which were green or blue depending on the color of her outfit, were full of humor. She loved color and dressed in a bright mix of hues and patterns. The more vibrant the colors the better, it seemed. "Color lifts the spirit," she would say to me. Her signature apparel included wildly patterned scarves, some hand-painted by herself. She wrapped them around her head, choosing them to complement her athletic suits, which she called "my uniform." "I dress to meet the day, ready to shake a leg," she would laugh. Indeed, she did meet each day with enthusiasm and courage, and repeatedly reminded me of the Arabic saying "*al- haraka baraka*" (movement is a blessing).

One day, I asked Ariadne if she would let me record her recollections of life in Egypt. She agreed after some coaxing, and what follows is her story.

Ariadne tells her story

My family lived in Egypt as if they were going to live there forever. There was never any thought of one day having to leave.

My father was born in Egypt and died when I was ten, so I never got to know him well. His father, my grandfather, was a businessman who came to Egypt from Romania after his first wife died. Finding himself a widower with three children to raise, he was not ready to stay alone or to stay in Europe. On a visit to Vienna, he met my grandmother, who was fifteen years his junior and had never married before. He proposed, she accepted, and they married and moved to Egypt. Business opportunities were plentiful and life was gentler than in Europe. They had another three children together, my father being the youngest.

My grandmother was very refined, and my grandfather was a self-made man. They were really quite different, even though both had Western cultural backgrounds. People say, "*Vive la différence*," and this certainly worked for them. They were happy.

My mother's father came from Russia, and her mother, like Father's mother, from Austria. At some point my maternal grandfather turned in his Russian passport for a Portuguese one. Why? I don't know, but I was told that he bought it. Later, we all took Greek citizenship. Isn't this the story of the Jews?

Father died of a stroke at the age of forty after a business trip to Britain. He was in textiles, wholesale. A year later, Mother married his friend, who was also a businessman in textiles. He was kind and generous, and became like a father to me and to my sister Edwina. My stepfather, like my father, was Romanian. He spoke French better than English, and we all spoke

French at home. He also had two children and we were all related because my stepfather's first wife had been Mother's sister. My stepfather died ten years after his wedding to Mother, strangely on the same day as Father. Mother was twice widowed on the same day.

My Father had two sisters, both living in Paris. One taught at the Sorbonne and the other was a doctor. Both married Frenchmen and had one son each. They all had to wear yellow stars identifying them as Jews, and all were deported and died in concentration camps. My father escaped this horrible fate because he had moved to Egypt prior to World War II.

How did my family come to be in Egypt? I will tell you.

The man who became my stepfather was the one who reached out to Father, as they had been friends and business partners in Romania. In Egypt they met and married sisters and thus, growing up, my sister Edwina and I had playmates in our cousins Saskia and Nina, Mother's sister's daughters.

Our two families lived on Rue Suleiman Pasha in downtown Cairo. My aunt and her family were on the third floor and we were on the fourth. There were two apartments to each floor, all spacious and high-ceilinged, with long windows and narrow balconies. We were near the famous Swiss patisserie Groppi, and loved to wander in and out, sampling chocolates.

Often, Saskia and I wore the same clothes, our mothers dressing us like twins. When Mother made me a dress, Aunt Cecile made one just like it for Saskia. Edwina and Nina were dressed differently, however, as Edwina was a tomboy and refused to wear the frilly dresses our mothers made for us. They said, laughing, that they tried to knead, pinch, squeeze, and cajole Edwina into a feminine mold, but failed. They finally left her to her own devices. Every now and again, though, they could not resist saying, "Remember, Edwina, you're a girl!" As it turned out, Edwina was gay and moved to Paris as soon as she could. She desired a lifestyle and freedom to express herself that were not possible in Egypt. So, Edwina was the first of us to leave Egypt, and in France she met Albertine, who was from Arles and moved to Paris, where she and Edwina lived as a couple. They shared many interests and enjoyed many years together until Albertine died, Edwina following soon after.

Mother and her sister were very close. Their husbands were close, too, and devoted to each other and to the wellbeing of our families. In fact, we were so close that, not only did we live in the same building, sharing daily visits, going on vacations together, we also shared our big American Buick and its driver. It was a 1940s model with a prominent grille on its front end that always made me think of a huge smile. As a toddler I apparently said to Mother, "*Shufi* (look), Boo-Ik is smiling." She laughed and said, "*Non, non, Ariadne, elle a une moustache*" (No, no Ariadne, she has a moustache).

My grandmother, Father's mother, mostly spoke German, and so we grew up speaking French and German. For some reason Oma, as we called her, despised Yiddish. Don't ask me why. My father knew Yiddish and teased her, saying, "You can despise any language you like, Mama, as long as you are *abi Gesunt!*" (healthy). She retorted, "*Ach*, don't speak this language in my presence!" I never found out why she so disliked Yiddish, which is a form of German, after all. She was Austrian to her fingertips, so could this have been snobbery? Was Yiddish not refined enough for her taste? Who knows?

Like our mothers, we were sent to a school run by German nuns, and then to French schools. For high school, at Father's insistence, we moved to British schools, as he believed that English was the language that would serve us best as adults. Of my school years, however, I remember little except for the snacks prepared by Oma that awaited us after school.

My grandmother, who lived with us, was a wonderful baker, especially of Viennese pastries and delicacies. She always had something delicious for us to enjoy with tea in the afternoon. My favorite was *apfelstrudel*. I also loved her *sachertorte*, which she made on special occasions, and for which I still have a recipe. In typical Viennese fashion, my grandmother grew up attending parties at home where guests danced the quadrille, the mazurka, and the polka. She recreated this European atmosphere and lifestyle in Egypt, Viennese delicacies and all.

Grandmother had only one sister left behind in Austria. She had married an Austrian Jew who converted to Christianity. My great-aunt refused to give up her Jewish identity, and in 1933 my uncle apparently announced that he was leaving to join the French Foreign Legion. She was left stranded with three children to raise in a Europe that was increasingly hostile to Jews. I can only imagine what a nerve-wracking time this must have been for her. My aunt fled to Sweden, taking her three children with her. They became refugees. She said, "We got away in time, anti-Semitic fervor nipping at our heels." She lived for a time in Stockholm while my family made arrangements for her and her children to join us in Egypt. When my great-uncle reappeared, he was repentant. I don't know if my great-auntie ever forgave him.

Why would a Jew join the Foreign Legion? I wondered, and always got the same answer: "He is not the only one." It is a peculiar story nonetheless. Apparently, there had been a Romanian Jew who joined the Foreign Legion to avenge the death of his family at the hands of a prison guard in the concentration camp where they were held. Father told the story with dramatic flair. It took years for this legionnaire to track down the murderer, and when he did, in Indochina, he killed him. Such stories did not explain my great-uncle, but had a hypnotic effect on me and the other children.

As my mother was growing up, the emphasis on education for girls was not great. Girls were expected to marry and raise families. They were trained primarily to run their households, to sew, make pastry, lead a life of leisure, and at most do good works—charity work, that is. Of course, in Egypt, many had servants who took care of everything. It was so in our family. We had a very easy life.

People traveled by boat in my grandparents' and parents' day, and in mine too. Mother said that sometimes someone would fall ill on board ship or give birth at sea and these people, landing in a port of call like Port Said or Alexandria, simply decided to stay. Egypt was a land of opportunity before the 1950s, when, sadly, the tide turned and it became dissatisfied with the Jews.

My father wanted us children to learn English because he harbored a dream of moving to England. Whatever his reasons, he could not convince Mother. She would not agree, saying they had a good life in Egypt. Why move? I overheard an exchange of words between my parents that Mother said she later regretted. Her refusal to accompany Father meant that he traveled alone for business, leaving us for long periods of time. When he returned, he tried again to persuade her to at least travel with him. She was unmoved. He did prevail in sending us to the English Mission College for the final years of our schooling, however—a small victory.

Father spoke English well. Mother did not speak it so well. She knew some Arabic, but it was negligible—kitchen Arabic, we called it. One day a servant came to Mother and said he had to go up to the roof, "'alashan a'mal zayy al-nas ya sitt" (to do as people must do, my lady). Mother was indignant. Because of her poor Arabic, she thought he was being insolent. "Imagine saying such things, Ariadne!" she exclaimed. I laughed and explained that the man was saying he needed a bathroom break but was requesting it in a delicate way. I was always proud to understand and be able to express myself in Arabic, unlike so many Europeans who looked down their noses at Arabic. In our family, we were not afraid of Egyptians, although later I developed a fear of them because of certain experiences and the mounting enmity they began to show toward us. The actions that led to our exodus were a far cry from the welcome we had received.

At school, I had Muslim and Coptic friends. It didn't matter to us what religion the other was. We were good friends, that's all. After leaving Egypt, though, I lost touch with all of them. Some of my Jewish friends, however, kept their contacts, and some even returned to Egypt to visit when it became safe again. Their returns were a form of pilgrimage. They went to places where they had lived, and visited what was left of the synagogues and the dilapidated Jewish cemeteries. Some wrote about their experiences in memoirs or articles.

When I was growing up, most of our servants were Egyptian. One, named Maro, was Armenian. Her family had been massacred by the Turks and she came to us as a girl. I don't know exactly how she came, maybe through an orphanage. She lived with us for ten years until she married, and then left to raise her own family. After Maro left, we had only Egyptian maids. My cousins Saskia and Nina had Italian maids because their father was better off than ours. Well, they were nannies, governesses really, not maids. We had a Sudanese cook and his helper, as well as a chauffeur, whom we shared with my uncle and aunt. They were all wonderful people. They were clean, hard-working, and loyal, for the most part. Only once did Mother have to fire one of our servants who turned out to be a thief.

We were steeped in European culture even though we lived in Egypt, and never thought of ever leaving it. We loved our lives in Egypt. We enjoyed some Egyptian foods, but the kitchen staff was mostly taught French and Viennese cuisine. They cooked one way for us and another for themselves. My cousins and I loved what the servants made for themselves and sneaked into the kitchen to beg a bowl of *fuul medammes* (fava beans) with *baladi* bread, or *kushari* (rice and lentils topped with crisp fried onions). Our family meals consisted of steaks, french fries, salads, sautéed vegetables, fish with mayonnaise, and so on. We lived side-by-side with Egyptians, but for the most part led separate lives.

My greatest love in Egypt was the Nile. I loved watching the opening and closing of the bridge to let boats through as we waited to cross the river to get to the Tawfiqiya Sporting Club. I also loved our excursions under sail on feluccas (boats with lateen sails). On full moon nights we took picnic baskets and sailed for hours. It was magical.

Mother was able to marry her sister's husband because Aunt Cecile had died a year prior to Father's passing. As they could not "live in sin," they decided to marry. This raised a hue and cry, with people whispering, "His wife has not even been dead a year," and so on and so forth. For Mother and Uncle Jacob it was a practical decision. I do think Mother was happier with him than with Father. I didn't mind him at all. In fact, he was good to Edwina and me, but Saskia was uncomfortable with the situation and never able to accept that my mother had replaced her own. Mother took Edwina and me to Palestine on holiday to give Saskia and Nina time to adjust. It was not yet Israel. We drove.

At home, we did not receive a profoundly Jewish education. We celebrated the feasts and got together as a family, but did not perform prayers in any regular way. The males of the family, however, wore their prayer shawls to Temple, especially for weddings. We celebrated Kippur at the temple and liked going there, particularly so we could meet our friends. Despite our casual approach to Judaism, we fasted on Kippur. I remember sipping lime juice with cloves in order not to faint from hunger. Edwina liked teasing me with mention of strawberry tarts and chocolate eclairs from Groppi.

When I married in 1950, it was in the Adli Street Temple, which was a Sephardic Jewish temple in downtown Cairo. Our Ashkenazi temple had burned down. Rabbi Nahum, the great rabbi of Egypt, officiated, along with a rabbi from the Ashkenazi community. One rabbi chanted, while the other rabbi recited according to our different traditions. I considered this a double blessing.

Mother retained two apartments even after Father died and she married our uncle. Edwina and I began using the empty one for political meetings and paramilitary activity. The grown-ups didn't know, and when they asked what we were doing, we said we were using the apartment to entertain our friends. In fact, we used the apartment to store arms. We had joined the Zionist movement and were already acting under the direction of the Haganah (Hebrew, defense), a quasi-military body that trained us in self-defense. I also joined the Maccabi, a Zionist youth movement established in Czechoslovakia in the 1920s to promote physical education among Jewish youth. I went regularly to meetings. As I attended an all-girls school, it was a way for me to meet boys. After a time, I was given the job of organizing activities for young girls because I had been a Girl Guide and had some experience. The year after we joined the Maccabi, we planned a trip to Palestine to work on a kibbutz, where there were boys and girls working side-by-side. There, I had my first taste of real freedom. I loved it!

At the kibbutz, which was near Haifa, we got up early to pick grapes in the vineyards. It was hot and we got sweaty, but I remember feeling such a great sense of joy. I shared a tent with other young people and discovered romance that summer. It was a happy time. After an arduous day of labor, we showered and attended lectures on Zionism. No one cared that it was hot and dusty. No one cared that the food was horrible. We were learning a lot and it was at that kibbutz that I learned to sing and dance. Edwina loved it too and would return to Israel regularly with her partner. That summer was our last summer together, however. She left for Paris immediately after.

I was not unhappy at home, but life in Cairo was limited and limiting. In the kibbutz that summer, I learned to breathe freely, fell in love with the Zionist movement, and became devoted to the idea of a Jewish homeland. At the end of our month at the kibbutz, our work was rewarded with an instructional tour of the country organized by the government of Israel. The first night, we slept in sleeping bags under the stars at Deganya, a very large kibbutz and one of the oldest. On Lake Kineret everyone jumped in to swim. It was magical.

Because we had never taken Egyptian citizenship, Edwina and I had traveled on forged passports, which we "borrowed" from a well-connected acquaintance who cautioned that they must be returned promptly as soon as we got back to Egypt. During our trip, the passports were lost and we were stranded. Because we were guests of the state they had to do something with us. They put us up in an empty schoolhouse, where we slept on the floor in sleeping bags and washed at a hose bib on an outdoor faucet. We had no money. It was dramatic! Meanwhile, the authorities helped us get in touch with our family. While Edwina found this an exciting adventure, I could not overcome my sense of panic. Would we ever get back? We were in a sorry state when our parents got to us: unkempt, undernourished, and so glad to be taken to the Eden Palace Hotel, where we bathed, put on fresh clothes, and gorged ourselves at the restaurant. We were allowed to rest for a few days before returning to Egypt.

In 1946, I became increasingly involved in the young Zionist movement. I was asked if I wanted to know more about the movement and joined the Haganah, a paramilitary group. The person who recruited me said, "There is a training class starting this summer. You can join, but don't say anything to anyone about your activities, not even your family." I agreed and was instructed to go to the Eglise Saint Joseph, a Catholic church founded in the nineteenth century, and to wait there for someone to pick me up. "A car will stop. Don't turn around or hesitate, just get in. We will take care of you," the anonymous contact said. The two men who came to get me explained more about the Haganah, saying that this organization, created to defend the Jewish people, was illegal and that I must be ready for dangerous work. He said, "If you are caught, it's death by hanging!" I responded, "I'm not afraid. I want to join."

Once I confirmed my intentions, I was taken to a dark room where I saw a Bible and a handgun sitting on the bare table. I was ready for my initiation. A man behind a black curtain spoke: "Swear that you will never betray us." I did, saying I would have my eyes put out rather than reveal the names of members or turn my back on the movement. It was all austere, dark, cloak-and-dagger. I felt I was living with a capital L!

I started attending meetings, not knowing much about the other members. Everything was shrouded in secrecy. That summer I returned to Palestine. It was all exciting and exhilarating. I felt my life bursting with purpose and righteous struggle. I was sent to a kibbutz along with other youths from Egypt. For five weeks our group received paramilitary training. I sent letters home describing how I lived in the midst of fields of flowers, tended chickens, milked cows, and so on. In fact, I was scaling walls, jumping over barriers, crossing lakes, learning to navigate a boat, to use knives, guns, explosives. I got up at four in the morning to train and learned to stay awake to stand watch. Then I was recruited to train others. It was arduous and the facilities provided were primitive. There was no plumbing. We used outhouses with corrugated iron roofs and holes in the ground for toilets. Needless to say, there was no hot water or electricity. We were nine hundred meters above sea level and it could get cold, but the views were breathtaking. We could see from a good distance the British military coming to inspect us, and therefore had warning and time enough to hide arms and stow away anything that would arouse suspicion. This was a year before the United Nations partition plan for Palestine. We were instructed to communicate minimally, and not at all with kibbutzniks. We followed orders.

In the course of that summer, I was bitten by a mosquito and contracted malaria. I was very sick. One of the kibbutzniks gave me his bed in a room with three boys. I slept all the time. There were no doctors, and in order to get a doctor to the kibbutz, mirrors were used to signal emergencies. Finally, a doctor was alerted and came from Deganya, the oldest kibbutz, founded in 1909. He arrived on the back of a donkey and said I should not be moved. I recovered. Despite the bout of malaria, I remember this time in my life as exciting. It was a time of great intensity and fervor, a beautiful time.

As soon as I could safely travel, I returned to Cairo, going back to my middle-class lifestyle. But I had tasted something different and I needed more. I volunteered in a clinic in the Jewish quarter of the city, Harat al-Yahud, in addition to attending classes. My mother and Uncle Jacob were unaware of my involvement in the Zionist movement and saw me as a young woman maturing and leading a student's life of study, sports, socializing at the club, or going out with friends. But my outings revolved primarily around the movement by then and included training to shoot firearms and grenades. These exercises were conducted in the desert. I practiced regularly and recruited others from Harat al-Yahud. The quarter was really a ghetto, its inhabitants leading very different lives from ours in downtown Cairo or Zamalek.

In the spring of 1948, I returned home one day from Harat al-Yahud, had dinner, and went to bed, as I was exhausted. At three am, we were awakened by a loud knock and found an officer of the police and his *shaweesh* (soldiers) standing at our door. "Ariadne Juran? We have orders to search your house." I was rattled, but had to let them in. They did and found a bombshell in the pantry, a remnant of World War I, clearly inscribed "Gallipoli, 1914–18." "*Kumbela!*" declared the officer in charge. "But it's just a souvenir," I countered. "Tell that to the *ma'mur* (police chief) down at the station," he replied. I was under arrest. Mother, Edwina, Uncle Jacob, Saskia, and Nina stood by in shock.

I was taken by taxi to an apartment consisting of three rooms. There were thirty-three women there already. I asked the guard in charge of us if I could have some cotton. She was sympathetic and brought me a wad covered in Mercurochrome and asked where I was wounded. I wasn't. My monthly cycle had started. At the time, shoulder pads were in vogue. They were sewn into jackets and even blouses. We all wore them to give our shoulders a broader look. I took mine out and used them as sanitary napkins. Other women gave me theirs as well. In hindsight it seems comical.

My fellow prisoners were a mix of Zionists and communists, and the friendships forged during the frightening days of our incarceration are some of the most intense I have experienced. Unlike the communists, we young Zionists were not at all prepared for prison. We did not know how to comport ourselves, we were ignorant of our legal rights, and we had never heard of the Geneva Convention. The communists tried to educate us. We had no lawyers. We were political prisoners and our parents didn't know what to do to help. So they did the only thing they could think of: They went to City Hall and asked for guidance. The answer they got was, *"istannu, isburu"* (wait, be patient). Families were beside themselves with worry. There was first and foremost the fear of not knowing. "How long will I be here? Will they hang me?" The physical conditions were terrible. It was hot, and the windows were boarded up so we could not communicate with anyone outside. The building was directly behind a poultry market and the stench was intolerable. I could not stomach chicken thereafter, and have become a vegetarian since. If I come within smelling distance of a chicken coop, even a clean one, I gag.

The communists educated us. One of them was our cellmate Lydia Harrari. She was brave, feisty, and unflappable. At the time of her arrest, she was a nursing mother, and of course her breasts were swollen and full of milk. What did she do? Lydia extruded her mother's milk regularly and made a sort of fresh cheese with it—Labna, she called it. She was an original. And she was an organizer.

One day, Lydia turned to us and said, "Did you know that under the Geneva Convention we must be given twelve piasters of food a day?" We gawked at her. She then called us to gather around her and asked, "Do you like the wormy feta cheese they are feeding us?" We all said we wouldn't touch it even if we were starving. What did we know? So Lydia said, "How about we strike and each demand a hard-boiled egg and yogurt with our bread?" We were in awe of her and chanted so the guards could hear: *"Aywa! Aywa! 'Ayzeen beid wa-laban zabadi! Aywa, Aywa, 'Ayzeen beid wa-laban zabadi, Aywa, Aywa ... "* (Yes, yes, we want eggs and yogurt). When we could not get a rise from the ranks, we started to shout, *"Ma'mur, ma'mur, 'ayzeen al-ma'mur . . . Ma'mur, ma'mur, 'ayzeen al-ma'mur!*" (Police chief, police chief, we want the police chief!).

"How long do we keep this up?" I asked. A few others chimed in with: "How long, Lydia, how long? How long, Lydia, how long?" It became a sort of refrain for our group. Humor helped us keep our spirits from flagging. One of our cellmates—whom we had nicknamed 'Aragoza' because, like the traditional puppet 'Aragoz,' she was sharp and funny—used foolishness as a weapon. She started in, dancing like Aragoz, brandishing a wooden spoon and leading us in a chorus of "Long live Lydia! Long live Lydia!"—a tribute to our champion. We laughed and felt the pall hanging over us lift a little. Nothing had changed but our attitudes. We were still captives in a horrible place, the outcome of our captivity unknown. Humor is an antidote to fear. It certainly was for this group of women.

Lydia stood up to answer our questions and said, "We will keep this up as long as it takes to get their attention, or die if we must!"

One of our cellmates said, "*C'est une force de la nature*" (She is a force of nature). Lydia was brave and we admired her and followed her lead. We continued chanting and stamping our feet. We called out, "*Ma'mur, ma'mur, ma'mur!*" and so on until he actually showed up and confronted our unruly and heat-withered gaggle. He raised his voice to be heard over the din of female voices demanding better food. Lydia then added, and we echoed: "*Iftah al-shibbak, iftah al-shibbak!*" (Open the window! Open the window!)

The *ma'mur* kept addressing us: "*Ya sittat, ya mazmazellat, al-sabr tayyib, al-sabr muftah al-faraj! Ya sittat, ya mazmazellat. . .*" (Ladies, young ladies, patience is good, patience is the key to deliverance). He was amused, and surprisingly gentle and respectful. When we quieted down, he agreed to send us better food, and the next day we had a hard-boiled egg and a small earthenware tub of yogurt with our bread. It was the same yogurt the milkman made and peddled door to door. The windows remained boarded, however. The communists continued to agitate for better conditions and visitation rights. As a result, my mother was allowed to visit me, and eventually we were allowed to receive packages of food from home.

One day, the *ma'mur* called for me and I was escorted to his office by a *shaweesh* (a low-ranking policeman). Before I went, Lydia coached me: "Remember, Ariadne, if he asks you a question respond only by giving your name. Say nothing else. Good luck!" I went with Lydia's injunctions ringing in my ears: "Don't say anything. Don't divulge any names."

The *ma'mur* greeted me and invited me to sit down. He said, "I wish to speak to you—" I interrupted him, stating my name as Lydia had instructed me to do. "My name is Ariadne Juran." He smiled. "I want to speak to you about your mother—" I cut in, "My name is Ariadne Juran." He started again: "Your mother—" I piped up, "My name is Ariadne Juran." Finally, he banged his fist down on his desk and said sternly, "Be quiet and listen!" I waited. "Your mother used to come and see you and bring you food. We don't see her anymore. Is she angry with you?" Oh my goodness, where was he going with this? I mellowed and said, "My mother is not angry. She comes, but she stays on the street." He said, "Well, she can come see you inside. We won't bother her." I was rendered speechless with surprise and must have looked so sheepish. He laughed.

When I got back to our cell, Lydia said, "What did they ask you? Did you do as I told you? Did you only state your name? Did they threaten you?" I said, "I was not threatened or tortured or anything, Lydia. He asked if I wanted to see my mother."

It was striking how differently we young Zionists were treated from the communists and Muslim Brothers in prison. Of course, we know of Zionists who were arrested, tortured, and hanged, but somehow it was different for us. Perhaps because we were women. We knew what the police could do, as we had seen the assassin of Nuqrashi Pasha, who had been led away and returned in a bloody state before he was hanged. To this day, I feel my stomach churn when I think of it. Strangely, we were not touched physically and when I got sick in prison, I was sent to a hospital under guard, in a taxi.

At the time I was escorted to the hospital, I was already engaged to be married. The *shaweesh* who escorted me knew this somehow, and asked, "Do you want to see your fiancé?" I did not answer and felt my body stiffen. He said, "I'm not asking anything in return. All I want is for you to know that Egyptians are not all bullies." I relaxed. I decided to trust him and told him where my fiancé worked and he took me to see him. It was an act of kindness I will always remember.

I was confined from May 1948 until December 1949. Once I was released from prison, I began wedding preparations. Rather, I found myself in a daze amid wedding preparations. Mother and other family members had begun to put together my trousseau even before my release and there was a frenzy of sewing, including, of course, sewing my wedding dress. I can barely remember the arrangements for our wedding dinner and dance, as I think I was still in a state of shock. I was married in the spring of 1950, and as Vinnie and I cut our wedding cake made by Groppi, I flashed back to my year of confinement and vowed never again to put myself in such a situation. I returned to a life of dancing, excursions to the Pyramids, dinners, movies, and family outings, but it all felt strange, like emerging into a too-bright light after darkness. Eventually, my eyes adjusted, so to speak, but life was never quite the same.

My husband, Vinnie, and I were blacklisted, suspected of subversive activity. Our phone was tapped, and we were followed, hauled in for questioning, released, and hauled in again. We started looking behind us whenever we left home and lived in fear of losing our freedom. Our concerns deepened once we had children. Whereas we had been intrepid and fearless as students involved in the Zionist movement, now as parents we had to think of our daughter, Marina, and our son, Enzio.

My sister Edwina had long before seen the writing on the wall and made her way to Paris, where she hoped we would one day join her. Destiny had other plans for us, however, and as we began to organize our exodus, we were arrested again and our children placed in hands of the Italian consulate. Arrangements were made for them to be cared for by Italian nuns, until a decision could be made as to their fate and ours. Meanwhile, we had no idea where they were. Imagine our agony!

A month after our capture, the Italian consul was allowed to visit us in prison. He informed us that our children were safe and sound, and that we would be reunited soon. First, however, we had to agree to sign over our assets and properties to the Egyptian government. We had to comply, and soon after were escorted to Alexandria, where we were handed our exit visas, as you could not leave Egypt without them at that time. We were informed that passage had been booked for us on a ship sailing for the port of Ancona on the Adriatic Sea. Enzio and Marina would be delivered to us on board ship. Since Vinnie carried an Italian passport, the children and I could be issued Italian passports too. Only after we boarded did we see that our exit visas were stamped "*bidun rugu'*," meaning return is forbidden. I was angry and disheartened, but there was nothing to do but look forward and pray.

On the eve of our departure, we were taken under guard from Cairo to Alexandria, where we spent a sleepless night. Early the next morning, we were perfunctorily handcuffed and led away. But where were the children? We stood on the pier until the men guarding us commanded us to get on board. We went up the gangplank feeling as if we were going to meet our executioners. We were wracked with fear and dread. Finally, from the deck we made out two tiny figures coming toward the ship. Instantly, I recognized Enzio by the way he was holding his teddy bear by the leg, while Marina clutched her doll with both hands. Vinnie and I wept with relief.

Our children, as it turned out, had been bundled up and placed on board a truck traveling on the desert road between Cairo and Alexandria. The Italian consul himself had entrusted them to a Jewish woman going to join her husband, who was in the same predicament as ourselves. Along with a few other refugees, they had had to travel under cover of night. They were being transported clandestinely. She told us when we met that the consul had said to her, "Signora, please take these two under your wing until you reach the pier in Alexandria. You will find their parents waiting on board the same ship as your husband."

Why, when we still had family in Cairo, were the children entrusted to the Italian consul? A cousin of Vinnie's, still in Cairo wrapping up loose ends before leaving for good to join his own family in Venice, offered to take them when he heard we had been arrested, but the consul advised him to leave it to him. "The children will be safest in our care," he said, and as the cousin knew him to be a man of his word, he deferred to the consul. And so this is how we ended up leaving Egypt forever, our children joining us just hours before the ship sailed.

Leaving Egypt for good, we were allowed only one suitcase each, the clothes on our backs, and twenty Egyptian pounds. The children took it all in their stride, but Vinnie and I traveled in a sort of fog. One day, a fellow passenger standing on deck with us said, "Did you know that there had been an important Jewish community in Ancona since the tenth century?" He added, "The first bishop of Ancona had once been the great rabbi of Jerusalem." We were surprised and questioned the veracity of this tale, but it turned out to be true. This rabbi had converted to Christianity and took the name Quincus.

This bit of information got me wondering about how the Jews spread throughout the Roman Empire in early times. Also, I wondered what it must have been like to wander for forty years in the wilderness. Some converted to escape persecution, but most endured. I know firsthand what it feels like to be expelled, to enter uncharted territory, to have to start over and never be able to go home again. The diaspora, the dispersion of our people from their homeland, resulted in the Jews of ancient times being driven from Israel to wander the world. With the State of Israel now a reality, would the Jews ever have to wander again? Daydreaming about our destiny as a people brought to mind Sukkoth, our festival commemorating the forty-year period the Israelites wandered in the desert. Every fall, in front of our houses, we used to set up open-air shelters, sukkahs, where we lived outdoors for seven days. We did this to remind ourselves that for the Jews, no home is permanent.

As soon as we arrived in Ancona, we were met by Israelis who waited on the pier for ships with Jewish refugees on board. They shouted greetings into their megaphones: "Welcome! Come home! Come to Israel! Come to us! Come to Israel! Come to us!" Vinnie and I were tempted. Had we not believed in the creation of a Jewish homeland and worked for the Zionist cause? Why not go to Israel and participate in the construction of this new nation? We debated, but decided to stay in Italy where we had family and could make a sure start. Perhaps one day, once we were established, we would go, we thought. Israel in those early days was a pretty rough environment and some people faulted us because they construed that we were shying away from hardship. One said outright: "You claim to be Zionists, yet you won't put your shoulder to the wheel to build our new homeland?" I could not argue, but remembered what a devout Jewish friend had once said to me: "The Book is my homeland." She meant the Torah. Her powerful statement has remained with me.

On the pier in Ancona, we were met by Red Cross volunteers who gave us coffee, brioches, and 10,000 lira to get started. We were given perfunctory lodgings until arrangements could be made to join our relatives in Venice, where Vinnie soon started a printing business. We remained in Venice until an opportunity presented itself for us to go to the United States. We went forth remembering what the Talmud says about how a person should be soft like a reed, not hard like a cedar. And so we looked forward and stayed soft. Like our ancestors, we were determined to bend, not break.

In the course of our journeys, I had purchased a pocket-sized notebook and began to collect sayings, proverbs, and meaningful quotes, which inspired my courage and my resolve to remain strong in the face of life's storms. On a scrap of paper, I had jotted down the lyrics of the song *You'll*

Never Walk Alone and pasted them into the notebook: "When you walk through a storm, hold your head up high, and don't be afraid of the dark . . . " Do you remember it?

Another notebook entry included a quote from Golda Meir, saying that to be a Jew was not merely a matter of religious observance and practice, but of pride in a distinct identity that has survived for thousands of years, despite trials and tribulations.

Yes, we too had experienced torment in our final days in Egypt, and yet we never felt we walked alone. Our faith and the solidarity of our community, along with the kindness of so many, sustained us. Our pain was not the fault of the Egyptian people. They were mostly gentle and friendly, even though some turned their backs on us in the end. True, some Jews reported being at the mercy of gangs of miscreants who took advantage of our ever-increasing vulnerability to inflict humiliation and harm. True, some Jews were arrested, tortured, and killed, but, for the most part, ordinary Egyptians did not lose sight of their humanity when the political atmosphere darkened. Even the officers who arrested us, and those who escorted us to the ship on our last day on Egyptian soil, were gentle. Their good hearts showed through their pretense of putting us under extreme pressure. I will never forget how they casually left our handcuffs unlocked, just dangling from our wrists, when escorting us to the Port of Alexandria for our final departure.

I would not have left Egypt had I been given a choice, and at the same time, I would not disavow Israel and the need for a Jewish state. We have been too badly hurt throughout our history as a people not to wish for a safe harbor, a place that's ours. Why is it that despite being a constructive presence everywhere we went, we still ran into so many who reviled us? Does it surprise you that the Jews longed to end their suffering, their wandering, and dreamed of a homeland to call their own?

My husband, who had studied the Torah, said to me as our exodus became imminent: "*Elleh mass'ei B'nai Yisrael* (Here are the journeys of the children of Israel). Didn't the Jews wander for forty years in the desert when they left Egypt led by Moses? It has been our destiny it seems, my dear Ariadne. We are travelers, our people scattered on every continent. Today, we are following in the footsteps of our forebears."

I retorted, "We are not following, Vinnie; we have been pushed over a cliff!"

He put his arm around me and said, "Think of us as roving ambassadors who take the best of our experiences and contribute our ideas, energy, and imagination to anywhere we land. This is an example of the steadfast wisdom of the Jews; maybe even our mission."

Jewish enterprise, tenacity, endurance, imagination, and wisdom have left significant marks everywhere Jews have lived throughout our history. Vinnie was right. We have wandered, often not by choice. We made a point of remembering the words of Maimonides, Jewish philosopher, physician, and scholar, who himself fled Spain to escape persecution and died in Cairo in the early years of the thirteenth century. He warned that a person should beware not to cast his thoughts backward for his eyes are placed on the front of his head for a reason. Father repeated a similar message as we were growing up: "Go forward. You are not meant to go backward. Look ahead where your eyes direct you!" We did.

We have been taught to remember and to recount the history of our people from generation to generation, and to remind others of our rich, complicated, often painful heritage. The Passover seder is such a time of remembrance, a time of great significance for us as a people. Rabbi Nachman said: "The Exodus from Egypt occurs in every human being, in every era, in every year, in every day." Our lives reflect this. As contained in the story of the Exodus, we can find our own stories, and we are still here to tell them.

Notes

1   Min Jin Lee, *Pachinko* (New York: Grand Central Publishing, 2018) 491, 493.
2   The capitulations system was put into effect in the nineteenth century, but as Egyptian nationalism grew, efforts were made to abolish this extraterritorial legal system of consular jurisdictions for foreigners. At the Montreux Convention in May 1937, an agreement was signed to fully abolish the system after a transition of twelve years and put foreigners under the jurisdiction of the Egyptian courts.
3   This mixing of languages is reflected in the book, where transliterations are commonly the author's own—intuitive, colloquial and not scholarly— recounted from conversations with her interlocutors as they switched between English, Arabic, French and Hebrew.
4   An old-fashioned expression, allegedly meaning to unburden oneself.